CONTENTS

CHAPTER 1

INTRODUCTION:

POLITICS AND ECONOMICS IN PUTIN'S RUSSIA: WHAT DO THEY MEAN FOR THE U.S. ARMY?

Stephen J. Blank

The five diverse chapters herein are papers presented at the Strategic Studies Institute's (SSI) IV Annual Conference on Russia that took place in Carlisle, PA, on May 15-16, 2012. They represent the first two panels of that conference, which examined politics and economics in Vladimir Putin's Russia. Despite their diversity of assessments and the varied subjects upon which they touch, the conclusions that they present are rather uniform in their pessimism concerning current and future trends in Putin's Russia. Readers will encounter here an immobilized political system that is essentially an archaic, neo-Tsarist, patrimonial, insular, even criminalized system where there is no rule of law, sanctity of contract, or guaranteed right of property, not to mention the civil and human rights we take for granted.

Moreover, the present leadership has already shown that it will not hearken to increasing public demands from below for reform. Instead, President Putin, in his new term, has shown an increasing willingness to engage in repression and actions that cannot even be called cosmetic reforms. These repressions, show trials, and farcically staged exhibitions of Putin's masculinity, new laws that are essentially decrees passed by what was once called an aggressively

1

obedient Duma, uncannily duplicate the same methods and procedures used by the Tsars after 1860 and the Soviet regime under Brezhnev from 1964 to 1982 when, in the wake of the great reforms, Russian society began to awake and demand still more reforms, and some brave souls even demanded revolution. The ruling regimes after 1860 were never able or willing to meet these demands and, for the most part, refused to make the necessary adjustments and reforms to survive and preserve Russia as a competitive great power. Ultimately, due to their failure to adapt to the requirements of a modernizing society and modernity in general, not only in terms of domestic political or economic progress, but also strategic competitiveness, these regimes found themselves increasingly deprived of internal legitimacy and authority and prone to enter into a series of wars, none of which they won, and some that were catastrophic, that led to their ultimate destruction in 1917 and again in 1991. Moreover, the Tsarist and then the Brezhnev regimes responded in much the same way as does the current government. Essentially, they all resorted to show trials, police repressions, occasional murders, incarceration of dissidents, and mounting corruption, while the engine of economic development and growth broke down. More recently, the Duma, with its aggressively obedient majority, is redefining the laws of treason that would criminalize any dissent. In a sense, this calls to mind Joseph Stalin's 1950 formal reintroduction (in anticipation of another great purge) of capital punishment, allegedly in response to the wishes of the Soviet intelligentsia. Or, they revive the earlier Stalinist practice of the 1920s and 1930s of drafting draconian and seeping decrees and laws to criminalize any behavior that the regime felt like attacking at any given moment.[1]

These same ploys characterize the resemblance of the current regime's policies to classic Tsarist, Soviet, and even Stalinist tactics and policies.[2]

Apart from the neopatrimonial and neo-Tsarist political system, with some important accretions from the Soviet period, we find an economy that also does not work and is becoming ever less competitive. By officials' own admissions, Russia today depends far too much on a cash crop (in this case, energy), again a resemblance to the Tsarist system that depended on agricultural exports and collapsed when they were either not possible, as in World War I, or when there was a global decline in the price of wheat. But the economy is inhibited not only by this structural backwardness, but also by the burden of enormous corruption. Russia is probably by far the most corrupt economy of the G20[3] and, in July 2010, the Association of Russian Attorneys for Human Rights issued a report saying that about 50 percent of Russia's $1.2 trillion gross domestic product (GDP) involves corrupt transactions.[4] This corruption has, if anything, worsened since then.

The pervasiveness and scale of such corruption affects the country's defense spending, where at least 20 percent of annual defense spending (if not 40-50 percent) is routinely stolen, misappropriated, lost, or just wasted.

> According to the Russian Statistical Committee, the volume of the shadow economy in Russia was 15% [of GDP] in 2012, whereas in [the] 1990s it was 22-23% of [the] (much smaller-SJB) overall economy. At the same time the Ministry of Economic Development estimated that the shadow economy contributed more than 50% of the population's income in 2011. The Federation of Independent Trade Unions stated that more than half of 2011 salaries paid in Russia were paid outside legal

channels. Viktor Zubkov, than Deputy Prime Minister, said that about a trillion rubles were taken out of Russia illegally in 2011 that corresponds to 4% of GDP and represents almost half of all money taken out of the country; it is almost equal the entire budget of the MVD (this would amount approximately $70 billion and the disparity with other reported figures show that officialdom has no exact idea how much is leaving the country except for the fact that the sums are enormous-SJB). Zubkov also estimated that about a trillion rubles was laundered in Russia in 2011.[5]

As one would imagine, such corruption has several profound consequences. It adds to the widespread preexisting disregard and contempt for the law and the culture of due process that is equally pervasive and reinforces arbitrary rule or what Russians call *Proizvol*. Second, it renders the country inhospitable to large-scale foreign and direct investment or even to investment by wealthy Russians who routinely ship money off shore before it comes back to Russia. Thus, estimated capital outflows in 2011 amounted to $85 billion.[6] Third, it demoralizes many potential younger elites who are already voting with their feet and leaving Russia. Fourth, in the defense sphere, it corrupts much of the country's overall national security policy, not least because it is clear that high officials are for sale, even to foreign interests.[7] Personal pecuniary interest, therefore, often trumps national interest, e.g., in key areas like arms sales or in the energy market. As a result, the temptation for these officials to engage in what might be called black operations, like running weapons to Iran, ultimately undermines the vital security interests of Russia itself.[8] Fifth, it deprives the economy of the capital needed for technological and military recapitalization, investment, and modernization, and thus consigns the country and millions of its citizens to greater poverty and incompetent or suboptimal goods and services than would otherwise be the case. Thus, even as Putin *et al.,* regularly state, in true Soviet and Stalinist style, that the defense industrial sector is the locomotive of technological progress, this sector cannot meet the military's needs, forcing Russia to buy weapons abroad from France, Germany, Italy, Finland, and even Israel. Worse yet, there are cases where the armed forces have refused to accept weapons produced for them by that sector, e.g., the Pantsir air defense system that Moscow also exports![9]

Meanwhile, the state sector has grown voraciously at the expense of the overall economy's growth potential, a fact that is not surprising, given the opportunities for personal enrichment through corruption with impunity. Thus, *The Economist* reported that during the past decade, the number of bureaucrats has risen by 66 percent from 527,000 to 878,000. The cost of maintaining this structure has risen to 20 percent of GDP.[10] Naturally, this phenomenon is accompanied by ongoing decay of infrastructure. In the late Soviet period, the government invested 31 percent of GDP; however, in the last 10 years, it invested only 21.3 percent, compared to China's 41 percent. Whereas the Union of Soviet Socialist Republics (USSR) built 700 kilometers (km) of railways a year, the present government only built 60 km in 2009. Similarly, the total length of paved roads in Russia in 2008 was less than in 1997, a sure sign of governance failure and misallocation of resources. As Zbigniew Brzezinski wrote:

> Informed Russian observers are also increasingly concerned that Russia's reliance on capital inflow in return for Russia's oil and gas is breeding a decline in the country's capacity to sustain technological innova-

tion and industrial dynamism on the global competition for economic preeminence. The renewal of Russia's industrial infrastructure, which in Soviet times was being replaced at an annual rate of 8 percent, has declined to 1-2 percent, in contrast to the 12 percent of the developed world. No wonder that the World Bank reported in 2005 that fuels, mining products, and agriculture accounted for 74 percent of Russia's total exports, while manufactures accounted for 80 percent of Russia's total imports.[11]

Consequently, Russia has recovered more slowly from the 2008 economic crisis than did the other BRIC countries (Brazil, India, and China). Since foreign direct investment (FDI) in Russia is a fraction of the total for the other BRIC members, 4.1 percent for 2007, that pace of recovery will probably not change anytime soon. Reportedly about 20 years behind the developed countries in industrial technology, Russia develops 20 times fewer innovative technologies than does China and devotes considerably less money to research and development than China does.

> Prime Minister Wen Jiabao of China, when visiting Russia in 2007, noted with satisfaction that Chinese-Russian trade in machinery products reached an annual level of $6.33 Billion. Out of politeness, however, he refrained from adding that $6.1 Billion of that sum involved Chinese machinery exports to Russia, leaving only $230 million of Russian machinery exports to China. Making matters worse, projections by the Organization for Economic Cooperation and Development for the year 2020 envisage not only China's gross domestic product as approximately four times larger that Russia's, but with India ahead of Russia as well.[12]

But the papers do not stop here. As Harley Balzer points out in Chapter 4, Russia's epistemic communities, i.e., communities of people who work with their minds like scientists, professionals, etc., remain trapped in a mentality that precludes learning from others and doing things differently than they have done for years, if not decades. This insular, corrupt, and self-perpetuating approach to research, development, science, technology, and education is a powerful factor in reinforcing the fetters that bind Russia and hold the country back. As Judy Holiday memorably stated in the movie, *Born Yesterday*, "This country and the institutions that govern it belong to the people who inhibit it." The insular, chauvinistic political system (ours is better, or in Russian, *nashe luchshe*) reinforces this proclivity to believe that there is no other way to do things other than what has always been done before, that Russia is uniquely endowed with a superior cultural-religious heritage, etc. Furthermore, these trends, as manifested in socio-political and economic action, only reinforce the tendency to repeat the same mistakes of the past in the misconceived notion that doing the same thing without meaningful reform will yield the desired results, if we only do it better this time. These pathologies, for that is what they represent, are no less present in the defense and defense spending sphere, as Stephen Blank demonstrates and as noted previously. Indeed, the huge spending increases on procurement allocated till 2020 are one reason why Finance Minister Alexei Kudrin broke with the government and warned about its policies.

The defense and security implications of this dysfunctional and archaic system are equally negative. Currently, there is a huge defense buildup that aims to spend $716 billion between now and 2020 to make the

Russian armed forces a competitive high-tech armed force, with 70 percent of its weapons being modern (whatever that category means to Moscow). Yet this system already has shown repeatedly that it cannot deliver the goods and that the attempt to remilitarize at this relatively breakneck speed (relative to other comparable powers) is failing to produce the weapons Moscow wants. Consequently, it is clear not only that nuclear weapons will remain the mainstay of Russian military might through 2020, but it is also equally likely, from the current vantage point, that this nuclear preeminence will remain well into the decade 2020-30 as well. This means that, for a whole range of contingencies, Moscow will have to rely more than any other comparable power on nuclear threats and deterrence, and deterrence presupposes a hostile relationship with the targets of that strategy. Apart from issues of democracy promotion and regional security in Eurasia, this conclusion has sobering implications for U.S. defense policy as a whole because it will place limits on what can be achieved through arms control treaties, obstruct the Barack Obama administration's declared ambition to move on to a zero nuclear weapons trajectory, and inhibit a genuine military and political partnership with Russia.

Furthermore, given the postulate presented here of a deteriorating domestic situation due to an increasingly sclerotic economic-political formation, we could well encounter a situation where a revolutionary situation inside Russia due to the blockage of progress intersects with a massive security crisis that could, as in 1991, involve a coup and the danger of seizure of nuclear weapons and potential wars across Eurasia. Or, we could see a diversionary war as the Russo-Japanese war was launched in part in order to busy "giddy minds with foreign wars." Arguably, we are witnessing the first signs in today's Russia of the advent of a long-term crisis culminating in such a domestic and then international crisis. This crisis would combine mounting disaffection, if not protest, and continuing subpar economic performance is a situation that approximates Vladimir Lenin's 1915 definition of a revolutionary situation. According to Lenin's oft-quoted definition:

> What, generally speaking, are the symptoms of a revolutionary situation? We shall certainly not be mistaken if we indicate the following three major symptoms: (1) when it is impossible for the ruling classes to maintain their rule without any change; when there is a crisis, in one form or another, among the "upper classes," a crisis in the policy of the ruling class, leading to a fissure through which the discontent and indignation of the oppressed classes burst forth. For a revolution to take place, it is usually insufficient for "the lower classes not to want" to live in the old way; it is also necessary that "the upper classes should be unable" to live in the old way; (2) when the suffering and want of the oppressed classes have grown more acute than usual; (3) when, as a consequence of the above causes, there is a considerable increase in the activity of the masses, who uncomplainingly allow themselves to be robbed in "peace time," but, in turbulent times, are drawn both by all the circumstances of the crisis *and by the "upper classes" themselves* into independent historical action.[13] (italics in original)

To be sure, none of this suggests the imminence of a revolution. Rather, it suggests the imminence of a structural crisis leading to the situation defined here by Lenin and which evermore characterized Tsarist Russia after the great reforms of the 1860s and the Soviet state after Leonid Brezhnev. Neither we, nor any other reputable observer, expect an imminent collapse of the Putin system. But Russia already appears to be visibly bearing the seeds of its own entropy and ultimate collapse. Distinguished Russian scholars like Lilia Shevtsova and Olga Kryshtanovskaya openly state that Russia has slipped into a revolutionary situation.[14] That process took some 50 years in Tsarist Russia and a generation in Soviet Russia, suggesting the acceleration of large-scale socio-political change and its growing department, even if we are talking about a long-gestating process. But if this assessment has merit, then we are only at its inception, not its conclusion, and many more negative phenomena and Russian behaviors can be expected before the advent of a crisis that could occur, if this acceleration of protest trends and institutional entropy occur by 2030. Potential contingencies could even possibly entail the use of force either at home (and not just in a counterinsurgency mode against jihadi rebels as in the North Caucasus) or beyond Russia's borders as in the Russo-Georgian war of 2008. Indeed, as the regime moves further along its current trajectory, such belligerent behavior increasingly appears to be the norm. As Andrei Illarionov, a former economic advisor to Putin, has observed:

> Since its outset, the Siloviki regime has been aggressive. At first it focused on actively destroying centers of independent political, civil, and economic life within Russia. Upon achieving those goals, the regime's aggressive behavior turned outward beyond Russia's borders. At least since the assassination of the former Chechen President Zelimkhan Yandarbiyev in Doha, Qatar, on 14 February 2004, aggressive behavior by SI (Siloviki-men of the structures of force-author) in the international arena has become the rule rather

than the exception. Over the last five years the regime has waged ten different "wars" (most of them
involving propaganda, intelligence operations, and
economic coercion rather than open military force)
against neighbors and other foreign nations. The most
recent targets have included Ukraine (subjected to
a "second gas war" in early 2009), the United States
(subjected to a years-long campaign to rouse anti-
American sentiment), and, most notoriously, Georgia
(actually bombed and invaded in 2008). In addition to
their internal psychological need to wage aggressive
wars, a rational motive is also driving the Siloviki to
resort to conflict. War furnishes the best opportunities
to distract domestic public opinion and destroy the
remnants of the political and intellectual opposition
within Russia itself. An undemocratic regime worried
about the prospect of domestic economic social and
political crises—such as those that now haunt Russia
amid recession and falling oil prices – is likely to be
pondering further acts of aggression. The note I end
on, therefore, is a gloomy one: To me the probability
that Siloviki Incorporated well be launching new wars
seems alarmingly high.[15]

Accordingly, even though no observer expects a
comparable revolution anytime soon, the signs of crisis are also quite visible for anyone who cares to look
for them. At the same time, the advent of social and
information technologies, as well as Russia's partial
integration into the global economy, suggests that any
repeat performance will take even less time than this,
so it is not inconceivable that within 10-20 years, we
could see a Russia openly enmeshed in a structural
crisis from which there is no way out other than large-
scale transformation, if not revolution.

Given Russia's strategic weight and military capability, this prognosis poses immense questions, if not
problems, for the U.S. Government as a whole as it

seeks to grapple with the realities of Russian policy. Were this a monograph on the subject of U.S.-Russian relations, it would take a long report to work through all those issues. But here, we must content ourselves with recommendations for the U.S. Army in its activities. To do that, we must view the Army in its current strategic context.

ASSESSMENTS AND RECOMMENDATIONS FOR THE U.S. ARMY

Any potential Russian crisis within the next generation will inevitably reverberate throughout the global system and with special force in Europe, Eurasia (the former Soviet Union), and East Asia. Moreover, that crisis will similarly and equally inevitably interact with indigenous crisis phenomena and trends, mainly in what used to be the Soviet south, i.e., the Caucasus and Central Asia (and potentially Ukraine and Belarus), if not in Europe. Indeed, a crisis in the former Soviet Union could ignite one in Russia. Central Asia and the Caucasus are already enmeshed in several actual or potential security challenges that can materially affect U.S. interests and partners, if not allies, for their own reasons—whether or not a crisis occurs in Russia. Furthermore, the advent of these crises in the Caucasus and Central Asia, or elsewhere, could, of their own accord, embroil the U.S. military and government (not just the Army) in their resolution. If they coincide with, trigger, or are the result of a crisis in Russia proper, the challenges to the U.S. Government and Armed Forces will be magnified commensurately, especially if nuclear contingencies come into play.

Unfortunately, these prospects, which are more likely than many believe, will catch the U.S. Army, the Armed Forces, and the government as a whole in the throes of a serious and possibly unprecedented strategic quandary. As many observers have noted, today the U.S. Army faces a situation where it has no declared enemy, no priority mission, and no clear concept of operations for any particular contingency that may occur. Whereas the Navy and the Air Force do have a concept of operations (but not a strategy) for overcoming enemy forces' anti-access and area denial strategies (A2/AD), namely air-sea battle, the Army has no such concept.

Moreover, and many commentators have missed this point, the air-sea battle concept is not exclusively reserved for an Asian-Pacific threat originating from China but could be employed, e.g., against Iran in the Straits of Hormuz. Or, in the event of a Russian attempt to take over one or more Baltic states, the United States and the North Atlantic Treaty Organization (NATO) would then have to resort to a European version of this concept of operations for the initial counterattack against such a Russian thrust. Neither is such a contingency purely notional, even though it remains a remote possibility for the immediate future. Moscow launched the first cyber strike ever attempted against a sitting government against Estonia in 2007 after a year of covert preparation, and Central European governments, particularly in the Baltic region, remain apprehensive about Russian intentions and capabilities in this region, which are rapidly being increased.[16] Neither can we take European or Eurasian security for granted. Russia has also admitted that it planned the Russo-Georgian war of 2008 beginning in 2006, thus publicly undermining all the pious statements about it having been attacked and was thus able to surprise key international actors, including the Georgian government.[17] Since Russian efforts to subvert European governments through "asymmetric" means, the linkage of energy, organized crime, intelligence penetration, political subversion, and military threats, specifically recurring nuclear and missile threats against all of Eastern Europe from the Baltic to the Black Sea states, are constant and unremitting. Since Moscow has shown its continuing addiction to aggressive actions in its neighborhood, complacency about European contingencies in the future is clearly unwarranted.[18] Such concerns must engage the strategic planner, especially one who is looking to events a decade or more from now.

But such observations about the European theater, not to mention the ever volatile greater Middle East or the increasingly volatile East Asian theaters, underscore the Army's and the U.S. Government's abiding strategic dilemma, which holds true whether or not Russia implodes or explodes a decade or so from now. That dilemma has two aspects. First, there is no visible strategy for either the Army or the other Armed Forces (merely listing missions and concepts of operations cannot, in this context, substitute for a true strategy). Second, as innumerable analyses and the current domestic crisis indicate, we are on the brink of strategic insolvency, with a defense establishment that cannot be maintained in its present form or size without radical and unpopular (to many constituencies) reforms.

While any Russian crisis greatly magnifies the challenges to U.S. power and interests, essentially, the Army finds itself obliged to say that no matter what kind of war ensues, it will go wherever the President orders it to fight (as if any other conclusion was thinkable) with whatever forces it has at the time. But it has no current or preexisting idea what the nature of that war is or an *a priori* concept of what goals it hopes to obtain in any particular theater.[19] It has no idea of what its strategic objectives are or should be, and neither do the other Services. All we have is a tactical or operational concept for the initial operation of gaining access to the contested theater. That hardly answers the requirement for strategy. This situation represents the antithesis of strategy and confirms the critical posture of many analysts, e.g., Colin Gray, that "All too often, there is a black hole where American strategy ought to reside."[20] As a result, critics have charged that the Army, in seeking to define for itself a strategic role, is "grasping for scenarios."[21] These scenarios comprise missions generally regarded as the core capability of the Marines or elite special operations forces like seabasing (operations that can be conducted without relying on infrastructure ashore) and counterproliferation missions.[22] To compound the Army's dilemma, there is a conspicuous lack of enthusiasm among political leaders in both parties, despite overblown campaign rhetoric, for sending it into another war anytime soon.[23] So, lacking a mission or a compelling strategic rationale or narrative, the Army starts from a disadvantage relative to the other Services, who have at least a concept of operations. But the Army's and the other Services' problems do not end here. Indeed, at the strategic level, they only begin here.

In the context of the larger framework of U.S. national security strategy, the air-sea battle concept comfortably fits with the concept of deterrence of major theater war that has stood at the forefront of U.S. strategy and policy since 1945. It is compatible either with the idea of deterrence by denial, i.e., deterring an enemy by making it clear that we will deny him a victory or with the alternative view of deterrence by punishment, namely raining down upon him so destructive a military force that, even if some sort of victory was temporarily achieved, the destruction wreaked upon him would far outweigh any such temporary or local gain. But that makes air-sea battle a concept that is optimally shaped for deterrence and for replying to a breakdown of deterrence. In other words, it is a concept of operations that is admirably shaped for the initial phase of a war. But being nothing more than a concept of operations, air-sea battle, as publicly described, suffers from serious defects. Given what we know about Russian nuclear strategy, the attempt to use air and sea power to rain down long-range strikes on Russian targets in, around, and immediately beyond the Baltic littoral almost certainly invites a retaliatory nuclear first strike by Moscow that will have an immediate and profound strategic effect, and not necessarily the one that Moscow counts on, namely its attainment of control over the ladder of intrawar escalation and a search for negotiations to forestall any further nuclear use. It is not too likely that Moscow would, however, opt for such a contingency, knowing that it would face this immense destruction for what are ultimately marginal gains.

In East Asia, as Ambassador Charles Freeman similarly observes:

> The evolving U.S. battle plan presupposes that, from the outset, any war that occurred (involving China in an offensive role—author) would involve U.S. strikes on forces and facilities on Chinese territory or immediately adjacent to it, This does not address the obvious difficulties of escalation control in these circumstances. Given China's possession of nuclear weapons, this plan is simply unrealistic.[24]

16

Likewise, Thomas Christsensen and Richard Betts wrote several years ago that:

> Thinking over the long term, however, it is hard to imagine how the United States could "win" a war to preserve Taiwan's independence against a resolute China. . . . Sinking the Chinese navy and defeating an invasion attempt against the island would not be the end of the story. Unless the U.S. Air Force were to mount a massive and sustained assault against mainland targets, the PRC would maintain the capability to disrupt commerce, squeeze Taiwan, and keep U.S. personnel at risk. As one American naval officer put it, "China is a cruise missile sponge." This will be doubly true once China builds more road-mobile solid-fuel missiles and learns better ways to hide its military assets.[25]

Thus air-sea battle could easily conceivably lead to an unpalatable strategic dead end but in the form of a much wider, prolonged, and desperate struggle with enormous stakes, where we will have fallen into that war with vastly insufficient forethought. The Napoleonic maxim, "*On s'engage et puis on voit*" (One commits himself and then looks around), hardly suffices as a guidance for contemporary strategic action. But the Army's lack of a viable concept of operations or mission for a breakdown of deterrence leaves it in precisely this situation, where it has a concept in search of a mission and a theater. Therefore, it cannot bring anything to the "table" concerning strategic missions, operations, or its enduring contributions to grand strategy, and the Navy's and Air Force's situation in this regard is hardly much better.

Neither do U.S. strategic dilemmas end here, for we are clearly confronting the overall problem of strategic insolvency, a dilemma that would undermine all existing strategic formulations, not to mention operational concepts like air-sea battle. We are already confronting this dilemma, even if there is no sequestration process as is possible as of October 2012.[26] Recent assessments of the new Asia-Pacific strategy pull no punches and state outright that the force structure being readied to implement that strategy is simply not sufficient to accomplish the mission. Congressman J. Randy Forbes (R-Va), Chairman of the House Armed Services Readiness Subcommittee, openly states that:

> The 'pivot' toward the Asia-Pacific region is a lofty objective, but maritime assets available to execute it — existing and planned — are simply not enough.[27]

Rear Admiral David Johnson, who supervises the Navy's submarine construction program, recently admitted that if "the price tag for building the newest vessels remains where it is today, there will have to be cutbacks to the *Virginia*-class (submarine) program," even though the Navy has already brought down those costs and is doubling its production from one to two subs annually.[28] Michael Auslin similarly argues that the Air Force's current budget is insufficient, given the range of missions and capabilities it needs to execute its strategic missions.[29] Likewise, a recent article observes that in Korea, we are unprepared for the real possibility of having to execute missions connected not just with a war there, but with a potential unification scenario. Although former Secretary of Defense Robert Gates stated that besides the capability to break down the door and win the air-sea battle, we must be able to restore a functioning government and society in war zones "and rebuild the house after war." The Army and overall U.S. military force required to do that mission is not the force that is either currently deployed in South Korea or that the United States has trained and ready to deploy, despite all our previous experiences in having to confront such requirements.[30] Finally, the recent study by the Center for Strategic and International Studies in Washington, DC, of the rebalancing of U.S. forces to the Asia-Pacific theater also pointed to substantial funding problems with regard to the new rebalancing.[31] These are only a few recent indicators of this insolvency in an ocean of commentary on this point.

Neither would all our problems be resolved if funding magically appeared. Our problems are as much, if not more than, strategic as economic. Arguably, the announcement of air-sea battle has ignited a new round in the Asian arms race. One can already see Japan, South Korea, and India substantially upgrading and modernizing their military capability and ambition to become major defense producers and even exporters. Russia, too, is already well into a huge modernization program of some $716 billion to reshape its entire force and develop a substantial conventional high-tech capability by 2020, and its apprehensions about China are poorly concealed.[32] Thus, it is entirely possible that continuing as we have been doing, assuming funding remains available, could bring about a continent-wide Asian arms race in conventional, and possibly nuclear as well, weapons that would merely aggravate the already high level of tensions in Asia and do nothing to stabilize the area or reduce the likelihood of military conflict. That is assuming funding is available. If it is not available, we may achieve a comparable effect but deprive ourselves of the means of dealing effectively with any violent contingency, if and when it occurred.

But beyond that, the Army, if not the other Services, also face deep cognitive challenges to their plans. This is a particular dilemma for the Army because many writers and authorities here and abroad believe that the main centers of future military operations will be in the aerospace, cyber, and naval — i.e., long-range strike — "theaters" and not land and traditional sea forces. Thus General Nikolai Makarov, Chief of the Russian General Staff, recently stated that:

> As you see, warfare center has moved to aerospace and information spheres, including cyber security, from traditional war theatres on land and sea. Concepts of network-centric war have made great progress.[33]

Makarov is hardly alone, either in Russia or here or elsewhere. Accordingly, the mantra of boots on the ground will hardly be convincing, even though the purveyors of short decisive victory through long-range strikes and high-tech have little to show for their many promises. Indeed, some adherents of better warfighting through technology have begun to realize that "our understanding of nonkinetic effects in cyberspace is immature."[34] In that case, a war with a large cyber dimension, or even with a significant though not preponderant one, could easily become quite unpredictable and even uncontrollable, not unlike the fears of what a nuclear war could become. So reliance on air, aerospace, naval, and cyber operations can hardly provide the basis for a reliable or reassuring warfighting strategy. Indeed, this brings us back to the dilemma postulated previously, namely, that current threat assessments fail to capture the highly complex future operational environment. Such a void leaves the Army (and to be accurate, the other Services, too) bereft of viable strategies for prosecuting war. Neither can the Army take refuge, as some have thought, in the idea that its future wars (whatever happens to the other Services) will be "murky irregular conflicts."[35] This is not just because the future is inherently unknowable. It also is true that it is a great fallacy to assume that the next war, even if it is an irregular one, will look like the current or last war. The Army, like it or not, must be ready for everything. Yet the pace of change is so swift and deep that the military is finding it difficult to understand what future advances in biotechnology and other weapons of mass destruction (WMD) scenarios might look like.[36] Undoubtedly, the same will be true for "murky irregular wars."

As one recent article observed, there is a wide range of actual or easily conceivable contingencies for which we cannot rely on Special Forces:

> Douglas Ollivant has also soundly observed that we cannot assume that special operations forces will be a salve for every security challenge we face. Some scenarios will simply be too big for SOF to handle alone. Even if the US does not seek to reconstruct collapsing states, securing weapons of mass destruction, and leadership targets in the aftermath of an implosion of Syria, North Korea, Libya, or any number of other states would be demanding tasks that special operations would have difficulty handling by themselves. Some sanctuary-raiding missions would require larger ground forces. Others may simply lend themselves better to general purpose forces. Recent African success waging combined land-amphibious operations in Somalia suggests that land forces executing amphibious raiding in Africa could inflict substantial damage on pirates and other foes. In other situations we may not be able to rely on proxies to do the job for us, either because of a principal-agent mismatch or lack of

capability. Finally, SOF and airpower in recent conflicts also depend implicitly on the enemy lacking the
ability to threaten the bases and supply networks that
sustain them with ground power, commando forces,
or long-range weapons. Should Afghanistan's government lose substantial amounts of territory or collapse
outright after US withdrawal, the basing arrangements
upon which we base our proxy warfighting would be
threatened.[37]

Moreover, even if the Army and the other Services
accept the need for comprehensive readiness across
the spectrum of conflict, it is still quite unclear how
the Army will operate in WMD contingencies, even
if it acknowledges their likelihood in the future.[38] At
the same time, the Army must be ready for all manner of combat operations ranging from contingencies,
where smaller units with fewer but better and better-
equipped army and joint forces engage the enemy,
up to and including large land battles of battalion or
brigade size, if not larger. Therefore, the Army must
formulate a compelling strategic argument that is not
just a service argument for more appropriations (as
one might suspect air-sea battle is) and that offers a
compelling enhancement of U.S. and allied security in
Europe and Asia, if not elsewhere.

TOWARD AN ARMY STRATEGY FOR EURASIA

The Army concept is one where the Army works
actively in peacetime with allies and partners to reshape their militaries and as part of overall U.S. policy
to reshape the strategic environment in Europe, Asia,
Africa, etc., to prevent wars from breaking out. While
this concept of shaping the theater during peacetime
to preclude or prevent war and build up allied and

partner capacity fully comports with deterrence by denial, as we saw in Georgia in 2008, it does not necessarily preclude a breakdown in deterrence or ensure that host country forces will be prepared for actual war that is imposed upon them. The Army and the U.S. military as a whole now recognize the need for more effective responses to the challenges of partnering with other militaries, including those in the former Soviet Union, to shape the environment and provide the basis for meeting contemporary global strategic requirements, as the characteristics of war change rapidly and assume a highly protean and dynamic profile. In the recent *Capstone Concept for Joint Operations: Joint Force 2020*, Chairman of the Joint Chiefs Army General Martin Dempsey observed that one of the eight key elements of anticipated global integrated operations is:

> *Fourth, globally integrated operations place a premium on partnering*. This allows expertise and resources existing outside the U.S. military to be better integrated in a variety of operational contexts. The complex security challenges of the future almost invariably will require more than the military instrument of national power. Joint Forces must be able to integrate effectively with U.S. governmental agencies, partner militaries, and indigenous, and regional stakeholders. This integration must be scalable, ranging from the ability of an individual unit to enroll the expertise of a nongovernmental partner to multi-nation coalition operations.[39]

This requirement, coupled with the other seven requirements for jointly integrated forces that are capable of conducting scalable operations involving multiple stakeholders listed there, comprise a major challenge to the Army under stretched budgetary conditions. Nevertheless, crisis denotes both challenge and opportunity. In the concept of the contingencies outlined here of a renewed crisis in Eurasia, if not elsewhere, due to a potential or even likely crisis, if not collapse, of Putinist Russia in the future, strategic contingency might open the way for an alert Army and other military leadership to see a way out the Army's present quandary.

What the Army and U.S. governmental elites must understand is that the argument presented in this chapter provides early warning of an impending, if not imminent, geopolitical crisis that could well morph into major strategic challenges. Indeed, Russian analysts themselves know well how precarious security is, particularly in the Caucasus and/or Central Asia, especially in view of upcoming U.S. and NATO withdrawal from Afghanistan in 2014. For example, the Valdai Club, a leading Russian think tank, recently wrote that:

> The entire Belavezha Accords system of state and territorial structure, which took shape as a result of the 1991 national disaster (the collapse of the Soviet Union in 1991), is illegitimate, random, unstable, and therefore fraught with conflict. The entire post-Soviet Eurasian space is an area with a complex combination of integration, separatist, and irredentist tendencies. The system has been in a state of permanent crisis for almost all of the 20 years since the collapse of the Soviet Union, and it is safe to say that in the future it is doomed to more or less conflict-ridden transformation.[40]

Such conflicts would almost certainly entail direct Russian military intervention, and the most threatened areas are those where the United States has now developed serious interests and partners, namely Central Asia and the South Caucasus. This analysis also naturally highlights the ongoing jihadi insurgency in the North Caucasus, for which Moscow has no credible strategy at present, not to mention the possibility of a "Falklands" scenario against Japan in the Kurile Islands, China's growing military power and contingencies associated with that trend, and the ever present pressure of the United States and NATO.[41] Neither is this just an unofficial think tank report. In 2010, the joint staff of the Russian-led Collective Security Treaty Organization (CSTO) stated that:

> The likelihood of conflicts arising on the basis of political, religious, ethnic, and other contradictions [in the former Soviet Union] is high, and it is impossible to resolve them without peacekeeping technologies.[42]

Western writers observe, too, that the peripheries of Eurasia like the South Caucasus remain regions at risk.[43] Given what we know of Russian military policy, it is quite unlikely that the CSTO or the Russian Army has yet acquired the relevant "peacekeeping technologies." Thus a crisis could break out here irrespective of what happens in Russia, and certainly Central Asian governments believe that such an outbreak is all too plausible after the International Security Assistance Force withdrawal from Afghanistan.[44]

There are further complicating factors in these peripheries, too. First, due to geopolitical and geo-economic shifts and the continuing, if not rising, criticality of energy and other raw materials, regions like Central Asia are increasing in geopolitical and geo-economic importance.[45] Second, in keeping with those trends, the peripheries are areas of visible, complex, but never ending great power contestation, not the least of which is Sino-Russian rivalry and collusion in constant probes against U.S. power, partners, values, and interests.[46] These probes continue in an effort to determine the scope and limits of U.S. power to defend partners and interests in the peripheries, and, if we fail to respond to these challenges, we and the targets of these probes pay the price. Thus Russian probes against Georgia in 2008 that met no U.S. resistance led to more threats, as did encroachments from the Chinese probes against U.S. naval vessels in the Pacific Ocean and South China Sea in 2009.[47] In addition, many of these probes or threats are not, at least initially, capable of resolution by means of U.S. conventional, let alone nuclear, weapons. As General James Cartwright, U.S. Marine Corps, then Commander in Chief of the U.S. Strategic Command, testified to Congress in 2007:

> While America possesses conventional capabilities second-to-none, we lack the capability to respond promptly to globally dispersed or fleeting threats without resorting to nuclear weapons. As good as they are, we simply cannot be everywhere with our general-purpose conventional forces and use of a nuclear weapons system in prompt response may be no choice at all.[48]

Since many of these actual or likely probes or crises that are expected in Eurasia regardless of events in Russia cannot and will not simply be met by U.S. forces for multiple reasons, we need to understand that we have now been given early warning and need to act accordingly. Meanwhile, if this is the situation in the peripheries as seen by both Russian and foreign authorities and experts, Moscow's own view of its domestic security situation (apart from the unresolved insurgency in the North Caucasus) is hardly one to inspire confidence. Clearly, the regime has good grounds for anxiety, as its own behavior shows. Russia's government labors under an enormous and constantly growing apprehension about domestic security that can only grow more, as does domestic opposition to it. Since 2005, the Russian Ministry of Defence formed Special Designation Forces from Spetsnaz brigades under the minister's direct control. They have air, marine, and ground components, and conduct peace support and counterterrorist operations.[49] Since the minister answers only to the president, essentially this also means putting all Russia under threat of counterterrorist or other so-called operations without any parliamentary accountability or scrutiny.

Since then, matters have, if anything, grown worse. An April 2009 report outlined quite clearly the threat perceived by the authorities. Specifically, it stated that:

> The Russian intelligence community is seriously worried about latent social processes capable of leading to the beginning of civil wars and conflicts on RF territory that can end up in a disruption of territorial integrity and the appearance of a large number of new sovereign powers. Data of an information "leak," the statistics and massive number of antigovernment actions, and official statements and appeals of the opposition attest to this.[50]

This report proceeded to say that these agencies expected massive protests in the Moscow area, industrial areas of the South Urals and Western Siberia, and in the Far East, while ethnic tension among the Muslims of the North Caucasus and Volga-Ural areas is not excluded. The author also invoked the specter of enraged former Army officers and soldiers who are now being demobilized because of the reforms might also take to the streets with their weapons. But despite the threat of this unrest, the government is characteristically resorting to strong-arm methods to meet this threat. In other words, it is repeating past regimes (not least Boris Yeltsin's) in strengthening the Internal Forces of the Ministry of Interior (VVMVD), and now other paramilitary forces as well.[51]

More soberly, this report, along with other articles, outlines the ways in which the internal armed forces are being strengthened. Special intelligence and commando subunits to conduct preventive elimination of opposition leaders are being established in the VVMVD. These forces are also receiving new models of weapons and equipment, to include armored, artillery, naval, and air defense systems. In 2008, 5.5 billion rubles were allocated for these forces' modernization. Apart from the already permitted "corporate forces" of Gazprom and Transneft that monitor pipeline safety, the VVMVD is also now discussing an *Olimpstroi* (Olympics Construction) Army, and even the fisheries inspectorate is going to create a special armed subunit called Piranha.[52]

Since then, even more information about the extent of the domestic reconstruction of the VVMVD into a force intended to suppress any manifestation of dissent have emerged. As of 2003, there were 98 special-purpose police detachments (OMONs) in Russia. By comparison, during the 1998 crisis of the regime and its elites under Mikhail Gorbachev, 19 OMONs were created in 14 Russian regions and three union republics. By 2007, there were already 121 OMON units comprising 20,000 men operating in Russia. Moreover, by 2007, there were another 87 police special designation detachments (OMSNs) with permanent staffing of over 5,200 people operating with the internal affairs organs, making a total of 208 special purpose or designated units with 25,000 well-trained and drilled soldiers. These forces, known as OMSNs, have grown from an anti-crime and anti-terrorist force to a force charged with stopping "extremist" criminal activity. All these units train together and have been centralized within the VVMVD to fight "organized crime, terrorism, and extremism." From 2005 to 2006, the financing of these units was almost doubled. By 2009, they were also working with aircraft assets, specifically the VVMVD own aviation center, with nine special purpose air detachments throughout Russia. Seven more such units are to be created. Furthermore, the VVMVD has developed a concept for rapidly airlifting these forces to troubled areas from other regions when necessary. These forces are also receiving large-scale deliveries of new armored vehicles with computers, in some cases, and command, control, and communications capabilities. Since these are forces apart from the regular VVMVD:

> On a parallel basis with the OMON empire, a multi-level internal security troop machine is being developed-with its own special forces, aircraft, armored equipment, situational-crisis centers, and so forth.[53]

When one considers this huge expansion of the domestic *silovye struktury* (power organs), it becomes clear why, in 2008, Russia announced that it would increase funding for the Ministry of Interior by 50 percent in 2010, and it becomes clear where the government's estimation of the true threat to Russian security lies.[54] If anything, things have gotten worse, and there also is now a spreading jihadist insurgency in the North Caucasus that is out of control and has recently launched operations in Russia's heartland, i.e., Tatarstan.[55] Therefore, neither the Russian government nor anyone else should take the durability of the current state for granted.

What, then, can be done under conditions of economic stringency and a true strategic fog?

ENDNOTES - CHAPTER 1

1. Ariel Cohen, "Putin's New 'Fortress Russia,'" *New York Times*, October 18, 2012, available from *www.nytimes.com*.

2. Simon Sebag Montefiore, "Please Hold for Mr. Putin," *New York Times*, September 22, 2012, available from *www.nytimes.com*.

3. The G20 is comprised of Argentina, Australia, Brazil, Canada, China, France, Germany India, Indonesia, Italy, Japan, Mexico, Russia, Saudi Arabia, South Africa, South Korea, Turkey, the United Kingdom, the United States, and the European Union.

4. "Report: Russia Perceived as Most Corrupt Major Economy," Voice of America (VOA), October 25, 2010, available from *www.voanews.com/content/report-russia-perceived-as-most-corrupt-major-economy-105774753/170290.html*.

5. Los Alamos National Laboratory in English, September 20, 2012, *Summary of Reporting on Russian & FSU Nuclear Issues–09/20/2012, Foreign Broadcast Information Service-Soviet* (hereafter FBIS-SOV), Los Alamos, NM: September 20, 2012.

6. "Russia Dumps Excessive Money: Capital Outflow Over $84bn in 2011–Kommersant," January 16, 2012, available from *www.cbonds.info/eng/news/index.phtml/params/id/544307*.

7. For example, Stephen J. Blank, "Civil-Military Relations and Russian Security," Stephen J. Blank, ed., Civil-Military Relations in Medvedev's Russia, Carlisle, PA: Strategic Studies Institute, U.S. Army War College, 2010, pp. 30-42.

8. "Global Alternative: The Logical Conclusion of a Major Failure of Russian Intelligence," Moscow, Russia, in Russian, November 9, 2009, available from *www.forum.msk.ru*, FBIS-SOV.

9. Ivan Konovalov, "Ground Forces Reject Pantsir: Antiaircraft system's Performance Unacceptable to Defense Ministry," Moscow, Russia, *Izvestiya Online*, in Russian, September 14, 2012, FBIS-SOV, September 15, 2012.

10. "The State of Russia: Frost at the Core," December 11-17, 2010, available from *www.theEconomist.com*.

11. Zbigniew Brzezinski, "Putin's Choice," *The Washington Quarterly*, Vol. XXXI, No. 2, Spring 2008, p. 109.

12. *Ibid.*

13. V. I. Lenin, "The Collapse of the Second International," available from *www.marxists.org/archive/lenin/works/1915/csi/ii.htm*.

14. Lilia Shevtsova, "The Next Russian Revolution," *Current History*, October, 2012, pp. 251-257, Shevtsova's paper in this collection; and "The Power Vertical: Russia's Revolutionary Situation," *Radio Free Europe Radio Liberty*, June 12, 2012, available from *www.rferl.org*; Jackson Diehl, "The Coming Collapse: Authoritarians in China and Russia Face an Endgame," *World Affairs Journal*, available from *WorldAffairsJournal.org/print/56631*.

15. Andrei Illarionov, "The Siloviki in Charge," *Journal of Democracy*, Vol. XX, No. 2, April 2009, p. 72.

16. Stephen Blank, "Web War I: Is Europe's First Information War a New Kind of War?" *Comparative Strategy*, Vol. XXVII, No. 3, 2008, pp. 227-247; European apprehensions were strongly voiced to the author by analysts and political figures during his trip to Warsaw and Helsinki in November 2011.

17. "Putin Admits Russia Trained South Ossetians Before 2008 Georgia War" - Transcript, President of Russia, August 10, 2012, available from *www.kremlin.ru*.

18. For examples, see Edward Lucas, *Deception: The Untold Story of East-West Espionage Today*, London, UK: Walker & Company, 2012; Edward Lucas, *The New Cold War: Putin's Russia and the Threat to the West*, 2nd Ed., New York: Palgrave Macmillan, 2009; Lada Roslycky, *The Soft Side of Dark Power: A Study in Soft Power, National Security and the Political-Criminal Nexus With a Special Focus on the Post-Soviet Political-Criminal Nexus, the Russian Black Sea Fleet and Separatism in the Autonomous Republic of Crimea*, Doctoral Dissertation, University of Groningen, Groningen, The Netherlands, 2011; Jakub J. Grygiel, Robert Kron, and A. Wess Mitchell, "Conclusion," *Navigating Uncertianty; U.S.-Central European Relations*, Washington, DC: Center for European Policy Analysis, 2012, p. 91.

19. General Raymond T. Odierno, "The U.S. Army in a Time of Transition," *Foreign Affairs*, May-June 2012, available from *www.foreignaffairs.com/articles/137423/raymond-t-odierno/the-us-army-in-a-time-of-transition*.

20. Quoted in Mackubin Owens, "Civil-Military Relations and the U.S. Strategy Deficit," February 2010, available from *www.fpri.org/enotes/201002.owens.civilmilitaryrelations.html*.

21. Kate Brannen, "Facing Uncertain Future, Army Reloads," October 4, 2012, available from *www.politico.com*.

22. *Ibid.*

23. *Ibid.*

24. Chas W. Freeman, Jr., "China's Rise and Transformation: Towards Pax Sinica?" *Washington Journal of Modern China*, Vol. X, No. 2, Fall 2012, p. 20.

25. Richard K. Betts and Thomas J. Christensen, "China: Getting the Questions Right," *The National Interest*, No. 62, Winter 2000-01, p. 27.

26. Clark A. Murdock, Kelley Sayler, and Ryan A. Crotty, " The Defense Budget's Double Whammy: Drawing Down While Hollowing Out From Within," Washington, DC: Center for Strategic and Internaitonal Studies, October 18, 2012, available from *www.csis.org*.

27. J. Randy Forbes, "Rebalancing the Rhetoric," *Proceedings of the US Naval Institute*, Vol. 138/10/1/316, October 2012.

28. Michael Welles Shapiro," Sub Cost Must continue to Fall, Admiral Says," *Newport News Daily Press*, October 19, 2012.

29. Michael Auslin, "The Air Force Needs More Dough; Make up $30B Tat Goes to Intel Agencies," *AOL Defense*, October 17, 2012.

30. Major Larry Sullivan (USAF), *Post-Unification Korea: Capitalizing on Opportunity,* Monterey, CA: Naval War College Press, 2012, pp. 12-13.

31. David J. Berteau *et al.*, *U.S. Force Posture Strategy in the Asia Pacific Region: An Independent Assessment*, Washington, DC: Center for Strategic and International Studies, 2012, available from *www.csis.org*.

32. Qichao Zhu, "Obama's Pacific-Pivot: the Coming Arms Race," *World Defence Journal*, No. 1, 2012, pp. 46-49; Stephen Blank, "The Chinese and Asian Impact on Russian Nuclear Policy," *Defense & Security Analysis*, Vol. XXVIII, No. 1, 2012, pp. 36-54.

33. "Russia Must Be Ready for Space, Cyber Wars," *Ria Novosti*, February 1, 2012.

34. Major General Brett Williams (USAF) "Ten Propositions Regarding Cyberspace Operations," *Joint Forces Quarterly*, No. 61, Spring 2011, pp. 11-17.

35. Major Phil W. Reynolds (U.S. Army) "What Comes Next? An Argument for Irregular War in National Defense," *Military Review*, September-October 2012, p. 35.

36. "U.S. Military Lags in Brainstorming Next-Gen WMD Dangers: Official," *Global Security Newswire*, September 2012, available from *www.nti.org*.

37. "Reinventing Landpower," *TRADOC Daily News*, October 5, 2012.

38. Steven Metz, "Strategic Horizons: Where the U.S. Military is Headed," *World Politics Review*, October 10, 2012.

39. Chairman of the Joint Chiefs of Staff, *Capstone Concept for Joint Operations: Joint Force 2020,* Washington, DC: U.S. Department of Defense, 2012, p. 6 (Italics in original).

40. Valdai Discussion Club Analytical Report, *Military Reform: Toward the New Look of the Russian Army*, Moscow, 2012, pp. 9-10, available from *www.valdaiclub.com.*

41. *Ibid.*, pp. 10-11.

42. Moscow, *Interfax-AVN Online*, in Russian, FBIS-SOV, September 21, 2010.

43. Richard Giragosian and Sergey Minasyan, "Recent Trends in Security and Stability in the South Caucasus," *Connections Quarterly Journal*, Vol. XI, No. 1, Winter 2011, available from *www. scribd.com/doc/101737289/Connections-the-Quarterly-Journal-Woiner-2011#page=72.*

44. Stephen Blank, *Central Asian Perspectives on Afghanistan After the US Withdrawal*, Central Asia Program, Washington, DC: George Washington University, 2012.

45. Kent E. Calder, *The New Continentalism: Energy and Twenty-First Century Eurasian Geopolitics*, New Haven, CT, and London, UK: Yale University Press, 2012.

46. *Ibid.*; A. Wess Mitchell and Jakub Grygiel, "The Vulnerability of Peripheries," *The American Interest*, March-April 2011; Stephen Blank and Younkyoo Kim, "Same Bed, Different Dreams: China's "Peaceful Rise" and Sino-Russian Rivalry in Central Asia," *Journal of Contemporary China*, forthcoming.

47. Mitchell and Grygiel.

48. Statement of General James E. Cartwright, Commander, United States Strategic Command, Before the Strategic Forces Subcommittee, House Armed Services Committee, March 8, 2007.

49. Zoltan Barany, *Democratic Breakdown and the Decline of the Russian Military*, Princeton, NJ: Princeton University Press, 2007, pp. 167-168.

50. "Russia On the Brink of Civil War," Moscow, *Vlasti*, in Russian, FBIS-SOV, April 19, 2009.

51. *Ibid.*

52. *Ibid.*

53. Iriana Borogan, "In Shoulder-Boards: The Kremlin's Anti-Crisis Project: When OMON Rushes to Help," Moscow, *Yezhenedevnyi Zhurnal*, in Russian, FBIS SOV, December 15, 2009.

54. Moscow, *Agentstvo Voyennykh Novostey Internet Version*, in Russian, FBIS SOV, July 4, 2008.

55. Stephen J. Blank, ed., *Russia's Homegrown Insurgency*, Carlisle, PA: Strategic Studies Institute, U.S. Army War College, 2012.

CHAPTER 2

RUSSIAN ECONOMIC REFORM 2012:
"DÈJÀ VU ALL OVER AGAIN"

Steven Rosefielde

INTRODUCTION

Russian economic reform is a perennial favorite, "a tale of two cities,"[1] where some see only past accomplishment and future glory, and others a "treadmill of Muscovite reform."[2] Therefore, no one should be astonished that discussions of contemporary Russian economic reform are "déjà vu all over again."[3] This does not mean that the two views are equally meritorious interpretations of Russia's economy and its prospects. There is only one correct view, and it is the "treadmill of Muscovite reform." The importance of the double vision lies elsewhere in the implacable political will in the Kremlin and segments of the west not only to deny the obvious, but also to depict tomorrow's Russian economy as the bluebird of happiness.

BLUEBIRD OF HAPPINESS

Official Soviet and Russian characterizations of economic performance and potential are persistently optimistic and used by some Western observers to paint rosy assessments of past accomplishments and future prospects. A single example will suffice. During the 1980s, official Soviet data (*goskomstat*) indicated that the Union of Soviet Socialist Russia's (USSR) gross domestic product (GDP) was growing more rapidly than America's, even though Mikhail Gorbachev acknowledged that the Soviet economy had been stagnant since 1978![4]

After Gorbachev decided to dissolve the Soviet Union on December 25, 1991, his successor, Russian President Boris Yeltsin, immediately launched a campaign for rapid democratization and economic transition (*demokratizatsia* and *perekhod*) aimed at transforming Kremlin rule from Communist party autocracy to democracy, and Russia's economy from central planning to free enterprise. Neither happened, but it became politically correct to say that they did.[5] Anders Aslund declared that Russia was on the express lane to capitalism in 1993,[6] to have become a "market economy" in 1995[7] and a "capitalist" system in 2007.[8] In 2004, Andrei Shleifer and Daniel Treisman congratulated Russia for becoming a "normal" developing country, including having made substantial democratic progress.[9] Their judgment was seemingly confirmed on December 16, 2011, when Russia agreed to join the World Trade Organization (WTO), pending formal Kremlin treaty ratification.[10]

The World Bank today portrays Russia as a democracy,[11] despite the objections of Anders Aslund[12] and Michael McFaul,[13] American Ambassador to Russia, and categorizes it as a MIC, that is, a "normal" middle income market country.[14] In its view, Russia weathered the global financial crisis of 2008 admirably,[15] and its prospects are favorable due to the Kremlin's "partnership" with the World Bank Group (including the International Bank for Reconstruction and Development, International Finance Corporation, and the Multilateral Investment Guarantee Agency).[16] Nonetheless, despite all these accomplishments, Russia's economy is said to be at risk.[17] It is vulnerable to budgetary constraints (nonoil fiscal deficit connected with expected declines in petroleum revenues) and long-standing structural issues, including the need to improve the investment climate significantly;[18] close large infrastructure gaps; diversify its export, tax, and broader economic base; improve governance; and strengthen institutions.[19] The World Bank contends that Russia's investment climate is poor, its infrastructure is laggard, its exports are excessively concentrated in natural resources, its tax and economic bases are too narrow, and its governance and institutions are weak.[20]

The World Bank asserts that Russia's leaders recognize these shortcomings and have responded by devising four broad economic reform initiatives to address: "Growth and Diversification, Skills and Social Services, Russia's Global and Regional Role, Governance and Transparency."

1. Growth and Diversification. Russia's economy is dominated by natural resource extraction undertaken by a few large corporations, a concentration reflected in its output and export structures and its fiscal dependence.[21] Recognizing this, the Kremlin has launched economic reforms to encourage "nonstrategic" small- and medium-sized enterprises,[22] and to increase the size of and modernize Russia's high-tech (e.g., the Skolkovo "innovation city")[23] and financial sectors.[24] This diversification not only will improve the structural balance, but also is intended to spur growth through the curtailment of state-owned enterprises and the rapid modernization of underdeveloped activities,[25] including innovation ("innovative Russia-2020").[26] These goals will be facilitated further by regional diversification ("Strategic Projects"),[27] improved public management,[28] enhanced business competition (achieved through better government regulation),[29] better financial management,[30]and infrastructural investment.[31]

2. Skills and Social Services. This is the second major category of the Putin regime's economic reform agenda.[32] The World Bank contends that Russia has made immense strides in the areas of universal primary education, equality for women, eradication of extreme poverty and malnutrition, lowering child and maternal mortality, and reaching very high levels of higher education enrollment. Putin's reforms will build on these accomplishments. Russia will strengthen its social safety net,[33] improve demographics and public health,[34] adjust education to provide a better mix of labor skills,[35] ameliorate inequality and social exclusion,[36] and soften interregional disparities.[37]

3. Global and Regional Role. The third major component of Moscow's economic reform agenda[38] includes initiatives facilitating economic integration in the Commonwealth of Independent States' (CIS)[39] ecological and environmental defense, especially in the Arctic. Globally, Russia is intensifying its international partnerships everywhere.[40]

4. Governance and Transparency. The fourth major element of Moscow's economic reform agenda[41] is important, especially improving self-government,[42] fighting corruption,[43] and achieving judicial efficiency.[44]

This survey reveals that Russian economic reform from the World Bank's perspective is mostly about routine policy and state regulation that are generically appropriate for any MIC, not market economic transformation. There is no core strategy, just a programmatic vision and promise that the government will do everything better. The World Bank's report, which parallels the Organization for Economic Cooperation and Development's (OECD) counterpart 2006 study, provides a valuable inventory of these initiatives[45] and makes the case for the proposition that Russia is on the fast track to becoming a normal country like America from a position of being a normal MIC with a fledgling democracy and rapidly maturing markets. It forecasts that Russia's GDP will grow at 3.5 percent per annum between 2012 and 2015.[46] Others holding similar views press this or that aspect of Russia's reform agenda reflecting diverse parochial interests but nonetheless adopt the position that the Vladimir Putin administration is moving forward with a progressive state regulatory and pro-competitive market agenda.

REALITY CHECK

The World Bank's inventory of Russian governmental economic reform programs and policies, although descriptively accurate, provides a misleading impression of the character and intent of the Kremlin's post-communist regime. Russia's government is anti-democratic, and its economy is organized for the benefit of privileged insiders, not the Russian people. The federation is no longer Communist, but this should not be construed as a radical break from Russia's hoary tradition. Its autocratic Muscovite rent-granting system has been in force continuously since the reign of Ivan III (The Great), Grand Prince of Moscow and Grand Prince of all Rus', in one form or another, since the 15th century.

The cornerstone of the paradigm is a particular type of autocracy, where the ruler is explicitly or implicitly owner of realm. The Tsar, General Secretary of the Communist Party, and now President (like the French absolute monarch Louis XIV), "is the law," with the power to act as he chooses, regardless of what he says. The autocrat can promulgate a constitution and impose administrative law (Catherine the Great), create a parliament (Nicholas II), install central planning (Joseph Stalin), and rule diversely with a unitary economic governance mechanism like rent-granting, the market, central planning, and regulation, or with a mixed regime.

Just before the Bolshevik *coup d'etat* in November 7, 1917, Russia had a tripartite economic governance system combining "rent-granting," (where the nobility and village communes oversaw agriculture, natural resources, and some industry in return for service, crop sharing, and taxes), state enterprise (tsar's estates, government enterprises, including weapons and luxury goods), and markets (based primarily on freehold ownership in low tech activities dominated by locals, and high-tech industries dominated by foreign direct investors).

The Soviets appeared to overthrow this order by criminalizing private property business and entrepreneurship (nationalization of the means of production and monopolizing state economic control)[47] and introducing central planning. However, rent-granting remained a powerful force, allowing "red directors" of all types to maintain the authority to use state resources with considerable discretion. On paper, the Soviet system seemed to be comprehensively directive, but, in practice, red directors were granted the privilege of operating the red Tsar's assets with munificent fringe benefits in return for service and a share of the usufruct, profits, and taxes.

Mikhail Gorbachev began the process of reverting to Nicholas II's mixed Muscovite model with his famous "perestroika" reform of 1987 (radical economic reform of the command planning system), which allowed leasehold proprietorships, markets, and entrepreneurship. Boris Yeltsin accelerated the process with his *perekhod* (transition) initiative, restoring freehold property ownership. This was promptly heralded as the beginning of a transition from communist authoritarian central planning to democratic free enterprise, but the judgment was premature. It was a post-royalist reversion to Nicholas II's Muscovite market assisted autocratic rent-granting, with a large dollop of state ownership in the military and natural resource sectors. Oligarchs became the new servitors.

Putin's government today, like Yeltsin's earlier, is a Muscovite autocracy organized for the benefit of privileged insiders, not the Russian people. The "people's assets" from the Soviet period were granted by Yeltsin to his favorites through various subterfuges,[48] creating the social foundations for the new post-Soviet Muscovy. The regime's predominant features are one-man rule and rent-granting, not democracy and market competition. This makes the regime intrinsically inefficient compared with the popular and consumer sovereign (neoclassical democratic competitive) model ascribed to Russia by the World Bank and radically alters real economic reform potential. The policies and reforms undertaken by the Kremlin and enumerated by the World Bank are merely efforts to enhance the efficiency of the Muscovite paradigm, not to move beyond it to democratic free enterprise. As a consequence, these endeavors can streamline and modernize a retrograde economic governance mechanism (including the public sector) but cannot Westernize it. They cannot make public programs responsive to the electorate or prevent the supply of goods in the private sector being primarily responsive to the demands of Putin and his "servitors" (oligarchs).

This judgment is confirmed by Russia's wretched economic performance from 1989 to 2012. Although, the way the World Bank casts the statistics, Russia's GDP doubled from 2005 to 2008 (18.9 percent per annum),[49] in reality, by using OECD data, the federation's per capita GDP was virtually flat for more than 2 decades (there was a hyperdepression during the interval).[50] This dismal assessment is easily confirmed by comparing the Central Intelligence Agency's (CIA) estimate of Russian per capita income in 1989 of $23,546 (adjusted to a 2011 dollar price base), which should be more or less the same today because there was little or no real growth point to point during 1989-2011, with the World Bank's contemporary figure of $10,500.[51] Obviously, the World Bank's picture of post-Communist Russian economic progress is amiss. If the CIA was right in 1989, Russian living standards have declined substantially since then, using the World Bank's contemporary estimate. Most of the discrepancy between the $23,546 and $10,500 figures is attributable to the CIA's exaggerated 1991 purchasing power parity estimates, but the point remains. Russia has not converged toward the developed Western standard of living under Yeltsin and Putin from the 1989 benchmark; it has diverged, falling further behind.

MUSCOVY AND THE WASHINGTON CONSENSUS

Muscovite rent-granting is a governance strategy used by Kremlin autocrats to create a cadre of loyal supporters by privileging the few to exploit the many. Muscovite rulers are primarily concerned with defending their realm and acquiring sufficient revenues to support the court and the power services (secret police and armed forces). They do not care if their servitors (contemporary oligarchs and other insiders), those subordinated to them, and peripheral players are inefficient as long as revenues are adequate, even though everyone is urged to do better. They do not care if servitors are overpaid, and everyone else is under-remunerated (Gini coefficient 42).[52] Servitors, for their part, are more concerned with obtaining additional rents from the autocrat than competitively maximizing profits. Like their liege, they prefer to enrich themselves through insider channels than competitively cost minimize and revenue maximize (profit maximization) in accordance with the neoclassical paradigm. Rulers and servitors often appreciate that democracy and free enterprise are better for the many but place their own well-being above the people's desires. This makes Muscovy intrinsically anti-democratic and anti-competitive, disclaimers to the contrary notwithstanding. History has demonstrated that autocratic rent-granting can be combined with state ownership, markets, central planning, and economic regulation without ceding sovereignty to the people or consumers, and this is the way that Putin has chosen to play the game. The approach is the antithesis of the Washington Consensus.[53] The programs, regulations, and reforms of the Russian government are primarily for the autocrat, not the *demos*, and improved competitiveness insofar as it is permitted serves the same purpose.

TREADMILL OF MUSCOVITE REFORM

The policies and reforms undertaken by the Kremlin in partnership with the World Bank Group can have positive results. Technology transfer and modernization in the public and private sectors, together with an expanded role for competitive markets, can improve productivity. The Tsarist, Soviet, and post-Soviet experiences, however, reveal that benefits are not automatic. The liberalization of Nicholas II's economy, including high tech foreign direct investment (FDI), had mixed results, mostly negative, as the Bolshevik revolution attests. The Soviet Union tried most of the World Bank Group's economic reform recommendations, including technology transfer and leasehold marketization. The result was stagnation and collapse. Yeltsin adopted the G7 transition strategy and immediately precipitated a decade-long hyperdepression. This time, of course, outcomes may be different.[54] Let us therefore provisionally accept the World Bank's forecast that Russia's GDP will grow 3.5 percent during the time frame from 2012 to 2015, a lackluster rate of advance given the country's relative economic backwardness. What precisely is there about Muscovite rent-granting that makes it productively inferior, unjust, and impervious to energizing reform?

The answer is simple. The Muscovite paradigm encourages rent-grantees to concentrate their attention on acquiring unearned incomes rather than creating value-added products or services, and it protects the privileged from competitive forces that might mitigate the harm rent-grant generates. Rent-granting is intrinsically underproductive, immoral, and corrupt from a neoclassical perspective, because it allows the privileged to receive income and wealth without earning them. Today's Russian "petrogarchs'" fortunes are tied more to currying favor with the Kremlin than efficiently managing companies and adding value. Other insiders receive state contracts without any obligation to perform, creating the semblance, but not the substance, of value-added (rent-fabrication).[55] The Muscovite system in this way offers an illusion of progress that masks its inefficiency and underproductivity. Corruption (privilege granting) in the Kremlin's scheme of things is not merely a matter of moral failure; it is the system's life blood.

None of this precludes Russia's privileged from trying to enrich themselves doubly by acquiring rents and maximizing profits; however, the regime's culture of corruption inhibits constructive impulses. The rent-seeking mentality keeps servitors' attention riveted on state handouts, with profit maximizing little more than an afterthought.

Adam Smith famously claimed that the potential losses caused by corruption, including conspiracies in restraint of trade, were less severe than might be anticipated due to the positive effects of moral self-restraint[56] and free competition (the invisible hand).[57] It is easily supposed that the defects of rent-granting are self-correcting, too; however, this does not follow because the Muscovite ethic is predatory, and the Kremlin is committed to creating privilege by deliberately suppressing competition. Putin has no objection to ordinary people competing among themselves and supplying services to the privileged at least cost, but any business that is lucrative can be or is taken over by the privileged and absorbed into the protected sphere. The same tactics are used in the Kremlin's dealings with foreign companies at home and abroad. Russia's Muscovite economy, consequently, is woefully inefficient. Labor is miseducated, misallocated, and underincentivized. Privileged companies do not profit maximize. They underinvest and misinvest, a problem exacerbated by the financial sector's misallocation of loanable funds. Foreign direct investors like

British Petroleum (BP) operate in treacherous waters and are routinely bilked.[58] Government regulation and programs are rent-granting activities, not handmaidens to market competition. The people's will is irrelevant, and consumers merely have limited market choice, not consumer sovereignty (their demand does not govern competitive supply).

The problem, of course, can be solved by the Kremlin voluntarily repudiating Muscovy or being forced to do so by a popular awakening, as many today seem to anticipate, but not otherwise. Better plans and regulations of the sort recommended by World Bank Group cannot compensate for the inefficiencies imposed by rent-granting, and, as the Soviet experience proved, they are inferior substitutes for markets.[59] Expanding the scope and competitiveness of ancillary markets should be beneficial, but this is precisely what Muscovy opposes to the extent that it leashes privilege. This is why Gertrude Schroeder's dictum holds undiminished. Russia is still on a treadmill of fundamentally futile reform.[60] Both the Kremlin's and the World Bank Group's nostrums are "Déjà vu All Over Again."

ENDNOTES - CHAPTER 2

1. Charles Dickens, A Tale of Two Cities, London, UK: 1859, Book 1, Chapter 1 - The Period:

> IT WAS the best of times, it was the worst of times, it was the age of wisdom, it was the age of foolishness, it was the epoch of belief, it was the epoch of incredulity, it was the season of Light, it was the season of Darkness, it was the spring of hope, it was the winter of despair, we had everything before us, we had nothing before us, we were all going direct to Heaven, we were all going direct the other way—in short, the period was so far like the present period, that some of its noisiest authorities insisted on its being received, for good or for evil, in the superlative degree of comparison only.

2. Gertrude Schroeder, "The Soviet Economy on a Treadmill of 'Reforms'," *Soviet Economy in a Time of Change*, Washington, DC: Joint Economic Committee of Congress, October 10, 1979, pp. 312-366.

3. "It's déjà vu all over again." Berra explained that this quote originated when he witnessed Mickey Mantle and Roger Maris repeatedly hit back-to-back home runs in the Yankees' seasons in the early 1960s.

4. Abel Aganbegyan, *Inside Perestroika: The Future of the Soviet Economy*, New York: Harper and Row, 1989.

5. Steven Rosefielde, *Russian Economy From Lenin to Putin*, New York: Wiley, 2007; Steven Rosefielde and Stefan Hedlund, *Russia Since 1980: Wrestling With Westernization*, Cambridge, UK, Cambridge University Press, 2008; Steven Rosefielde, *Russia in the 21st Century: The Prodigal Superpower*, Cambridge, UK: Cambridge University Press, 2005.

6. Anders Aslund and Richard Layard, *Changing the Economic System in Russia*, Hampshire, UK: Palgrave Macmillan, 1993.

7. Anders Aslund, *How Russia Became a Market Economy*, Washington, DC: The Brookings Institute, 1995.

8. Anders Aslund, *How Capitalism Was Built: The Transformation of Central and Eastern Europe, Russia, and Central Asia*, Cambridge, UK: Cambridge University Press, 2007; Anders Aslund, *Russia's Capitalist Revolution: Why Market Reform Succeeded and Democracy Failed*, Washington, DC: Peterson Institute of International Economics, 2007.

9. Andrei Shleifer, *A Normal Country: Russia after Communism*, Cambridge, MA: Harvard University Press, 2005; Andrei Shleifer and Daniel Treisman, "A Normal Country," *Foreign Affairs*, Vol. 83, No. 2, 2004, pp. 20–39; Steven Rosefielde, "An Abnormal Country," *The European Journal of Comparative Economics*, Vol. 2, No. 1, 2005, pp. 3–16.

10. "Ministerial Council Approves Russia's WTO Accession," Geneva, Switzerland: World Trade Organization (WTO), December 16, 2011. The Russian Parliament ratified WTO accession on July 21, 2012.

11. World Bank, *Country Partnership Strategy (CPS) for the Russian Federation*, Report No. 65115-RU, November 2011, p. 2. Another version of the same document is entitled *Russian Federation - Country Partnership Strategy for the period 2012-2016* (English).

> According to the 1993 Constitution, Russia is a democratic federal law-governed state with a republican form of government, comprising 83 federal subjects.

> The next parliamentary elections will be held on December 4, 2011, to be followed by presidential elections on March 4, 2012. President Dmitry Medvedev came to power in March 2008 and appointed Prime Minister Vladimir Putin. This ruling tandem has operated well since then. According to recent polls, the approval ratings for both the president and prime minister remain high, albeit lower than in 2010. The ruling party, United Russia, dominates the State Duma by holding 315 seats. The 2011 parliamentary elections will be the sixth in the history of modern-day Russia. Vladimir Putin announced that he will run for president. According to latest public opinion polls, the political situation is not likely to change significantly after the elections, with the four leading parties retaining their dominance in the Duma.

12. Anders Aslund, group email, December 12, 2011. Nonetheless, Aslund remains hopeful that democracy will triumph soon.

> Yet, I think Putin and his regime were effectively finished on December 10. I do not think it possible for Putin to serve as the next president, and I also think that Medvedev has no future role to play. Common slogans are directed against Putin: 'Russia without Putin,' 'Putin is a thief,' 'Putin to prison,' and 'out with Putin!' Both the Russian people and authorities have shown that Russia is ready for a new democratic breakthrough.

13. Obama administration's Ambassador to Russia, Michael McFaul, expressed his view that Putin's authoritarianism soon would give way to democracy. See Michael McFaul and Kathryn Stoner-Weiss, "Mission to Moscow: Why Authoritarian Stability is a Myth," *Foreign Affairs*, January/February 2008. McFaul worked for the U.S. National Security Council as Special Assistant to the President and Senior Director of Russian and Eurasian Affairs. McFaul is one of the architects of the "reset." See Leon Aron, "A Tormenting in Moscow," Washington, DC: American Enterprise Institute, April 12, 2012.

14. World Bank, *Country Partnership Strategy (CPS) for the Russian Federation*.

15. *Ibid.*

Russia has weathered the global crisis well despite the massive oil and capital account shocks. This was mainly because of the large pre-crisis fiscal reserves and fiscal surpluses that allowed the Government to mount a large countercyclical stimulus package in support of the financial system, enterprises, and households. Despite a large drop in real GDP in 2009 (-7.8 percent), an acute liquidity crisis, and a sharp increase in unemployment, the crisis was managed without systemic bank failures, and the economic and labor market conditions began to improve during 2009 in line with the rise in oil prices and the recovery in domestic demand and credit. Large increases in public sector wages and pensions cushioned the impact on the middle class and the poor, making the social impact less severe than it would otherwise have been. With the cyclical demand recovery in the global and Russian economies as well as energy commodities, Russia's real GDP grew 4 percent, and unemployment fell 2 percentage points from its peak during the crisis to 7.2 percent at the end of 2010.

16. *Ibid.*

Following a cyclical recovery of oil prices, economic activity, and employment during 2010, Russia's current macroeconomic situation remains favorable. After a 4 percent growth in 2010, the Russian economy continues to expand in an environment of declining unemployment (6.5 percent in July

2011) and inflation, rising domestic consumption, and still high oil prices. All sectors of the economy are growing, and domestic consumption — while less buoyant than anticipated — increasingly acts as an engine of demand growth. With good harvest and favorable food price outlook, annual inflation is expected to end at around 7.5 percent in 2011, somewhat higher than the Government's target of 6-7 percent but lower than at any time in recent years. The federal budget was anticipated to be in near-balance in 2011. A large current account surplus of almost U.S.$70 billion significantly exceeds the deficit in the capital account, which will allow the Central Bank to accumulate additional reserves.

17. *Ibid.*

Yet the risks to the global economy are growing and so are risks to Russia's growth. Reflecting the slowdown in major developed economies, and rising risks associated with the European debt crisis during the summer of 2011, the WBG's outlook for Russia's real GDP growth was revised to 4 percent in 2011 (down from 4.4 percent earlier in the year), and to 3.8 percent in 2012. This is predicated on the lower oil price outlook for Russia (Figure 2) [see original] and the global economy growing at more moderate rates, especially high income countries.

18. "Economic Policy Reforms 2012: Going for Growth," Paris, France: Organization for Economic Cooperation and Development (OECD), 2012.

The narrowing in March 2011 of the list of activities of strategic importance performed by non-state-owned banks removed the need for prior government approval for foreign acquisitions in this sector. Tariffs for selected agricultural products were reduced in response to the food price shock resulting from the drought in the summer 2011.

19. World Bank, *Country Partnership Strategy (CPS) for the Russian Federation.*

Beyond this favorable short-term picture lie heightened vulnerabilities of the Russian budget and long-standing structural issues. First, there is the large non-oil fiscal deficit of about 11 percent of GDP, compared with the sustainable 4.5 percent level. Second, with much smaller fiscal reserves than before 2008, Russia's budget is now more vulnerable to a new, sustained drop in oil prices. Third, Russia faces major structural problems in the medium term, including the need to significantly improve the investment climate, close large infrastructure gaps, diversify its export, tax, and broader economic base, improve governance, and strengthen institutions.

20. Finally, on the structural reform front, the Russian economy is facing multiple, long-term challenges. These include, first and foremost, improving the investment climate, addressing the large infrastructure gaps, diversifying Russia's tax, export, and broader economic base, and strengthening governance and institutions. In each of these areas, Russia scores comparatively low on many measures of performance, especially for a very large middle-income country aspiring to achieve high-income status within the next decade. These challenges underpin the Government's broader modernization agenda and the ongoing broad consultative discussions about the country's revised *Strategy 2020*. The extent to which these long-term challenges are met will determine the longer-term dynamics of the Russian economy, its catch-up with developed countries, and its ability to improve the living standards of its citizens.

21. World Bank, *Country Partnership Strategy (CPS) for the Russian Federation.*

The dominant concern for Russia's economic model remains the dependency on fossil fuel production and exports and the associated challenge of using hydrocarbon revenues effectively and efficiently. Russia is a global energy powerhouse. It is the world's largest exporter of natural gas and the second largest oil exporter. Energy resources combined with stronger social and economic policies have resulted in rapid social and economic progress during 2002-2008 and allowed it to weather the global crisis well. At the same time, however, as in many other major hydrocarbon producers, these resources are also the source of many of its development challenges. Relative to its structural endowments and trade potential, Russia appears to be under-exporting. Only approximately 9 percent of total exports in 2009 were accounted for by high-tech exports, mainly from the defense industry. There has been some shift to services over the years but the economic structure is dominated by large corporations with concentration in natural resources and low value added industries, while contributions from the SME sector are limited. The financial sector remains underdeveloped in terms of its capacity to mobilize and intermediate savings and is vulnerable to fluctuations in commodity prices and capital flows. Capital markets are inadequately developed and gaps exist in the oversight of the banking system.

22. Russia has a lengthy list of "strategic" enterprises, both military and key suppliers to the military, that prohibit foreign participation. Military industrial enterprises are all nationalized. "Strategic" enterprises essentially are state controlled. The number of strategic enterprises has not been reduced, nor is there any officially stated intention to do so. See OECD, "Economic Policy Reforms 2012: Going for Growth."

23. *Ibid.*

24. *Ibid.* "An April 2011 legislative act requires that all draft legislation be subject to regulatory impact analysis in order to identify the provisions that create unjustified obstacles to investment."

25. World Bank, *Country Partnership Strategy (CPS) for the Russian Federation:*

Russian businesses are often inefficient and tend to operate at low levels of technology and knowledge. Russia's product base has narrowed considerably over the past decade. In manufacturing, value-added per worker is similar to that of workers in China and India, but when labor costs are accounted for, overall productivity is lower. State-owned enterprises are present in more sectors of the economy than in any OECD country bar Poland. These enterprises also account for around 17 percent of total employment. Competition and the institutional and policy framework provide insufficient pressure or incentives to stimulate innovation. A difficult environment for the financial system leads to deficiencies in new company formation. External know-how transfers are limited with gross FDI inflows from 2005-2010 averaging a low 1.5 percent of GDP, with only 21 percent of these funds going to non-energy manufacturing.

26. OECD, "Economic Policy Reforms 2012: Going for Growth."

The Government's new innovation strategy "innovative Russia-2020" emphasizes the importance of private sector innovation activity. The creation of the Kolkovo "innovation city" may facilitate innovation, but its special legal and tax regimes go against the principles of universally applied rules and incentives.

27. World Bank, *Country Partnership Strategy (CPS) for the Russian Federation*.

Russia, as the largest country in the world by land area, faces significant challenges in development of its regions as average numbers for the country mask huge regional variations. Large and dynamic cities with high growth rates such as Moscow and St. Petersburg are highly congested and create substantial problems for urban transport management, while outside these cities poverty levels and unemployment can reach significantly high levels. According to Rosstat, the average level of unemployment from November 2010 to January 2011 varied from only 1.4 percent in Moscow to 47.5 percent in the Republic of Ingushetia. Headcount poverty rates (2008) ranged from 38 percent in Kalmykia (in the south) to 7.4 percent in oil-rich Khanty-Mansiysk.

Providing access to infrastructure of comparable quality is a principal development objective of the Federation, yet is also a significant challenge given its huge size.

Three strategic projects, including a Pacific oil pipeline, a drilling rig and an auto plant have been launched in the Far East.

See "Strategic Projects to Boost Russia's Far Eastern Economy," January 5, 2010, available from *www.chinaview.cn*.

28. World Bank, *Country Partnership Strategy (CPS) for the Russian Federation*."

Russia has a strong interest in continuing to improve efficiency and effectiveness of public financial management. Among other measures, the Government already introduced a three year budget framework, implemented legal and institutional mechanisms for monitoring sub-national public finance and Treasury principles of budget execution, created budget authority at the municipal level, and adopted legislation on insolvency of budgets of the regions. In late 2010 and 2011, Russia experienced large oil windfalls. Rising public expenditure commitments—including on the military, public sector wages, and pensions—are threatening to undermine fiscal and overall macroeconomic stability. The Government needs to substantially improve its long-term fiscal position by rationalizing public expenditures, managing the effects on public finances of an aging population, creating fiscal space for productive infrastructure spending, returning to an explicit fiscal rule, and broadening the tax base.

29. *Ibid.*

The Government has renewed and stepped up efforts to improve the business environment. Over the past few years these efforts have included the reduction of the burden of regulatory compliance on business, particularly in dealing with licensing and inspections at the subnational level, systematic monitoring of business environment indicators at the level of the regions, strengthening the enforcement of competition regulations, automating key administrative processes concerning business (e-filing of taxes), and stemming the proliferation of new regulations through the introduction of regulatory impact assessments. Despite the promising recent initiatives aiming at improving the business climate, perception indicators of the business environment remain poor. Russia ranks 120th among 183 economies in the 2012 Doing Business report. Government efforts now focus on streamlining key regulatory processes (e.g., issuance of licenses and permits) and monitoring administrative corruption affecting business at the level of the regions, where most regulatory processes occur. See further details in Annex 3.

30. *Ibid.*

The Russian Government is prepared to address existing weaknesses in the financial system. Prudential and non-prudential supervision requires strengthening through an improved regulatory framework in line with the G20 objectives. In particular, the Central Bank of Russia needs supervisory powers for several areas to mitigate banking sector risks. Also, financial system assets are concentrated in the banking sector where loan quality may be overestimated and the level of provisions is still lower than it should be. The breadth and depth of the equity, bond and investment fund markets remain well below capacity. Russia's capital markets also face deficiencies in market infrastructure (clearing and settlement) and a small institutional and retail investor base. The issues in the banking system and capital markets mean that there are problems in access to finance. The lack of access to finance is an obstacle for micro, small and medium firms, but is a particularly significant obstacle for medium and large firms. Structural obstacles to an enhanced access to finance remain to be addressed.

31. *Ibid.*

The Government regards infrastructure as a key development constraint with estimates for necessary investments at about US$1 trillion until 2020. According to a joint Bank/IFC study, Russia's potential energy savings are roughly equal to the annual primary energy consumption of France. Russia's transport infrastructure is generally poor and has been declining because of underinvestment in maintenance and rehabilitation. Major weaknesses are evident in the quantity, quality and institutions of several large infrastructure sectors. Upgrading Russia's infrastructure would require not only significant investments but also a strengthening of the country's institutional framework. Russia's environmental management suffers from poor governance and sometimes obsolete management practices. Environmental quality and control are poor for a majority of Russians living in the country's population centers. This has detrimental effects not only for those peoples' well-being but also a significant negative impact on Russia's economy.

32. *Ibid.*

The Russian Federation has made significant achievements in social and human capital development. The most notable achievements are in the areas of universal primary education, equality for women, eradication of extreme poverty and malnutrition, lowering child and maternal mortality, and reaching very high levels of higher education enrollment. With these achievements, the Russian Government is increasingly focusing its strategies on moving Russia closer to the level of achievements of other G8/OECD countries. In light of these ambitious goals, despite the impressive achievements to date, Russia is facing new challenges that will be critical to address if the government goals under the updated Strategy 2020 are to be achieved.

33. *Ibid.*

While general poverty levels have fallen sharply since the early 2000s, vulnerability to poverty remains a concern. Poverty rates are declining but remain significant with more than 18.5 million Russians living in poverty in 2010. Chronic poverty is now at about 7 percent, but the relatively high vulnerability to poverty affects about a quarter of the population (some 37 million people) 3. Efficiency in social spending, better targeting of social programs, as well as new transfers will be of critical importance in the future, especially with Russia's efforts to reduce the fiscal deficit and its exposure to changes in oil prices. Social protection is the largest budget item (55 percent) within the social expenditures4. Up to one quarter of social support beneficiaries are not poor. Furthermore, some of the social programs are suffering from low quality and weak integration with active policies that will bring people into jobs and out of poverty or social care. As Russia continues to develop, social transfers and programs will take up an increasing share of the national budget as in other OECD countries. Thus, enhancing its efficiency will be paramount as will be improving the quality of care and social programs.

34. "Since January 2011, citizens have got the right to choose a primary care doctor and an insurance company within the mandatory health insurance system," OECD, "Economic Policy Re-

forms 2012: Going for Growth; World Bank, *Country Partnership Strategy (CPS) for the Russian Federation:*

> Demographic and health trends are characterized by low fertility, high adult mortality and morbidity rates, and inefficient health spending, in addition to a rising pressure on pensions. The demographic profile of the Russian Federation shows a shrinking and aging population. Average male life expectancy in Russia is only 62.8 years (13.8 years less than the EU average), as opposed to 74.7 for women (7.9 years less than the EU average). The excess mortality is overwhelmingly attributable to cardiovascular diseases, cancer, alcohol poisoning, as well as injuries due to traffic accidents. According to Rosstat estimates, the working age population size will decrease by 10.4 million between 2011 and 2025, which is a major challenge for the Russian economy. Labor force shortages are expected to be compensated through labor immigration. Progress has been made in the fight against AIDS/HIV and TB. Still, Russia is among the 10 countries with the highest multi-drug resistant TB burden in the world. Furthermore, the Russian health system suffers from poor quality and inefficient spending with limited resources flowing to preventive care and an excessive amount of resources going to the hospital sector. Despite these challenges, Russia's total health expenditures is only 5.4 percent of GDP compared to an OECD average of 8.8 percent. Health indicators generally remain low in an international perspective and when compared to countries with similar levels of development. Given the relative low retirement age and the aging population, the fiscal burden arising from pensions will continue to grow.

35. World Bank, *Country Partnership Strategy (CPS) for the Russian Federation:*

> Skill mismatches in the labor market are turning into an increasingly important development constraint. Professional education and the renewal of skills for labor market entrants as well as existing workers are critical for adopting new technologies, diversifying the economy, and improving productivity levels. The latest EBRD-World Bank Business Environment and Enterprise Performance Survey (BEEPS) ranks skills as the number one concern for businesses in Russia. This is further exemplified by the fact that excess labor

market capacity appears to have been exhausted. Combined with the changes to the demographics of the Russian population, this indicates a serious and tightening bottleneck in the economy with regard to the provision of skilled workers, the quality of higher education and the renewal of skills within the existing labor force. Labor force shortages resulting from demographic trends make the Russian economy dependent on immigrant labor. The Russian Government is undertaking steps to attract more highly skilled immigrants to the country and is currently developing a scheme of organized recruitment of migrant workers. During 1999-2007, Russian GDP grew by an average of 7 percent annually with labor productivity growing an average of 6 percent per year accounting for 2/3 of the expansion in per capita GDP. Both female and male employment rates are below the EU average. The Russian Government is aware of the challenges which are to be addressed in the updated Strategy 2020. See further details in Annex 4.

36. *Ibid.*

The country's strong economic recovery and downward poverty trends belie significant challenges of inequality and social exclusion. Since Russia began its transition from a planned economy to a market economy some 20 years ago, economic growth has been steady and GDP per capita has increased threefold. Inequality as measured by the Gini coefficient rose significantly, however, from 28.9 to 42.2 between 1992 and 2009. Social stresses have been similarly magnified. Given that federal spending on social services in 2007-2008 already accounted for about 17 percent of GDP, or half of total federal spending 6, and was further increased by around 1.3 percent of GDP in 2009 and 2.2 percent of GDP in 2010, effectively addressing the issues of inequality and social exclusion will require an alternative preventative approach that can tackle the root causes of these issues.

37. *Ibid.*

The sharp disparities in development and living standards among Russia's regions require a differentiated policy approach. Russia's achievements conceal huge variations among regions in the level of social spending and poverty rates. For example, 82 percent of preschool education is financed through local government budgets, and therefore poorer regions will be more disadvantaged in their capacity to finance preschool education than richer regions. Substantial differences among Russia's regions are also apparent in per student spending and in the quality of education at the primary and secondary education level. Finally, vulnerable children including those with mental or physical disabilities and those who are infected with HIV suffer from educational exclusion. Addressing these variations among the regions across the human development spectrum will be critical for maintaining the path of achievements and calls for a more differentiated approach to policies and interventions.

38. *Ibid.*

Russia's national choices have critical impact on regional and global challenges. Russia is one of ECA's regional engines of growth, both as the major destination of exports and migrant labor from the CIS countries. The Russian Government wants to support economic integration within the CIS, including the creation of a common migration space and common labor market, but also has to grapple with social integration and adaptation of labor immigrants. The Russian territory contains about 22 percent of the world's undisturbed ecosystems. These have global value and significance for biodiversity protection, carbon storage and sequestration, and other critically important environmental functions. Strengthening forestry governance and management is particularly critical. The country's forests are at risk from forest fire, pest and disease outbreaks, and low rates of reforestation. Further strengthening of the national system for weather forecasting, hydro-meteorological services and climate monitoring remains a high priority for the Government as the impact of climate change is expected to increase the frequency of extreme and hazardous weather events. Due to the large-scale economic development and climate warming in recent decades, Russia's remote Arctic areas have become more accessible, resulting in a significant increase in human activities. This has led to more pressures on the pristine but fragile environment in the Arctic zone.

39. *Ibid.*

At the ECA regional level, Russia has become a prominent emerging donor. Over the last CPS period, it has implemented an ambitious development assistance program with significant contributions. With the approval of 75 percent of the population according to a 2010 WBG-managed opinion survey by the Levada Center, Russia will focus its assistance on LICs and lower-income MICs in ECA where it has many social and economic ties, and will also become active in other LICs. As a member of the Eurasian Economic Community, it initiated the establishment of a regional multilateral mechanism (EurAsEC Anti-Crisis Fund) administered by EDB to help deal with crisis related challenges in affected EurAsEC countries. Russian lead agencies have developed an understanding of the complexity of development aid communications and a sense of urgency for more active work in ensuring adequate information in support of Russian development aid. The Russian Government now plans to create a stronger institutional framework for development aid. It wants to set up a new bilateral development aid agency and enhance capacity within existing public agencies through better staffing, increased staff training, and development of expert potential.

40. *Ibid.*

At the global level, Russia has made important steps toward deeper integration into the international community. Russia is already a member of the G8, G20, and APEC. It is also making significant progress toward becoming a member of the OECD and the WTO. To reach its full potential as a prominent member of these global institutions, the Russian Government would like to employ the whole array of available policy instruments. Yet, with regard to the area of global public goods, where Russia is showing special interest in decisive issues like financial stability and food security, the Department for International Financial Relations in the Ministry of Finance is understaffed and the Government needs to strengthen the institutional structures and technical expertise necessary to provide effective leadership.

41. *Ibid.*

In recent years, the Government of Russia has completed or initiated a number of major reforms in the public sector. These efforts were intended to ensure sound management of public resources, create a more favorable business environment, and enhance public service delivery. Still, many challenges remain. Annex 5 analyzes recent developments and their impact, the main challenges, and the Government's current strategies for improving public sector governance.

42. *Ibid.*

Improving effectiveness and efficiency of public administration has been a high priority for the Russian Government in the last decade. The Government has undertaken a major effort to clarify and delineate functions between levels of executive government and establish local self government. The Government also launched a broad set of public sector reforms in areas such as civil service, budget process, and public administration. Some of these reforms, however, were only partially implemented and are not fully visible to the average citizen. The reforms are yet to translate into tangible and noticeable improvements in the quality and effectiveness of public administration in the eyes of the citizens and businesses. Government functions and civil service staff kept growing between 2004 and 2010. Government regulation is seen as excessive and often ineffective. Public services are heavily embedded in traditional administrative arrangements, which often encourage corruption and are burdensome for citizens and businesses.

43. *Ibid.*

Corruption has been recognized as one of the major obstacles for investments and growth. In response, the Government has embarked on a comprehensive anti-corruption program. Anti-corruption efforts have received new impetus in recent years under the leadership of President Medvedev. A Federal Anti-corruption Law and National Anticorruption Plan have been adopted and civil servants are required to declare their assets. Surveys of corruption perceptions show that Russia continues to lag relative to the ECA region and in global terms. The Government has made reform of the state contracting systems a key priority. Reported unofficial payments to obtain public procurement contracts were relatively high (BEEPS 2008), with 30 percent of firms reporting having made such payments, amounting to an average 11.5 percent of the value of the contract. Some improvements have been made, including introducing e-procurement through a single government portal, and according to Rosstat, competition in public procurement tenders has increased (average number of bidders in electronic auctions increased from seven in 2007 to 26 in 2009).

44. *Ibid.*

The judiciary is viewed as weak despite some improvements in recent years. Some high profile court cases have caused international concern about the full independence of the criminal justice system. However, according to surveys by the Levada Center, citizens' confidence in the courts rose from 45 percent in 2006 to 64 percent in 2010. According to the latest Business Environment and Enterprise Performance Survey (BEEPS), the share of firms using the legal system increased from 27 percent in 2005 to 43 percent in 2008, while only 3 percent of the companies surveyed reported corrupt practices. Two areas stand out for continued state attention in the judicial system: (i) continuing the trend towards greater transparency and efficiency in the functioning of courts (through investments in information technology and disseminating information to citizens on judicial decisions and the functioning of courts), and (ii) strengthening the enforcement of judicial and administrative procedures through the bailiff system, ensuring efficiency, transparency and integrity.

45. OECD. *Economic Surveys: Russian Federation 2006*, 2006.

46. World Bank, *Country Partnership Strategy (CPS) for the Russian Federation*, p. 52.

47. Private freehold property was criminalized throughout the Soviet period. Leasehold property was briefly permitted from 1921 to 1929 under the New Economic Policy for businesses employing 20 or fewer workers, and then reintroduced with few restrictions under Gorbachev after 1986.

48. Rosefielde and Hedlund, *Russia Since 1980.*

49. "In the period since 2005, the per capita GDP of Russia doubled to approximately $10,500 in 2010." The year 2008 is used as the endpoint in the text because Russian per capita GDP was

lower in 2010 than 2008. World Bank, *Country Partnership Strategy (CPS) for the Russian Federation*, p. 47.

50. West Europe includes Austria, Belgium, Denmark, Finland, France, Germany, Italy, Netherlands, Norway, Sweden, Switzerland, and the United Kingdom. GDP for West Europe and Russia is calculated in 1990 international Geary-Khamis dollars. See Angus Maddison, Historical Statistics, Groningen, The Netherlands: Groningen Growth and Development Centre, available from *www.ggdc.net/maddison/Historical_Statistics/horizontal-file_03-2009.xls*.

51. Steven Rosefielde, *Efficiency and The Economic Recovery Potential of Russia*, Surrey, UK: Ashgate, 1998, Table S1, p. xxii; CIA, *Handbook of International Economic Statistics*, CPAS92-10005, September 1992. Russian per capita income valued in 1991 dollars was 15,631. The inverse of GDP deflator 1991-2011 is 1.5. Russian 1989 GDP in 2011 U.S. dollar prices is $23,546. See *www.economagic.com/em-cgi/data.exe/fedstl/gdpdef+1*.

52. *Russia-CIA World Factbook*, 2012.

53. John Williamson, "Democracy and the 'Washington Consensus'," *World Development*, Vol. 21, No. 8, 1993, pp. 1329–1336.

54. Carmen Reinhart and Kenneth Rogoff, *This Time is Different: Eight Centuries of Financial Folly*, Princeton, NJ: Princeton University Press, 2009.

55. This was an aspect of the notorious phenomenon of hidden inflation during the Soviet era.

56. Adam Smith, *The Theory of Moral Sentiments*, London, UK: A. Millar, 1759. His attitude reflected the values later called the protestant ethic and an enlightenment reverence for the righteousness of pure reason. Muscovite autocrats would have scoffed.

57. Adam Smith, *Wealth of Nations*, London, UK: W. Strahan and T. Cadell, 1776.

58. Stephen Blank, "Is Russia Riding to BP's Rescue?" *Huffington Post*, October 25, 2010.

59. Steven Rosefielde, *The Impossibility of Russian Economic Reform: Waiting for Godot*, Carlisle, PA: U.S. Army War College, 2012.

60. Schroeder.

CHAPTER 3

ECONOMIC REFORM UNDER PUTIN 2.0: WILL PETRODOLLARS SUFFICE TO KEEP THE SHIP AFLOAT?

Stefan Hedlund

During his brief stint as caretaker of the Kremlin, Dmitry Medvedev succeeded in inspiring a great deal of hope about a different future for Russia. He went on record saying most of the right things, and he demonstrated his modernity by doing so in the country's new-fangled social media. If nothing else, Medvedev will surely be remembered as Russia's first genuine Twitter president.

With Vladimir Putin back in the Kremlin, however, a distinct sense of familiarity is again beginning to spread. Medvedev is fading into the background and may soon have dissolved completely, akin to a lump of sugar thrown into a cup of coffee. It is tempting to suggest that the impact of his one-term presidency will turn out to have been no more profound than that of his Twitter postings. But would that be correct?

The true test of the quality of Medvedev's legacy will rest in whether the dreams and visions that were associated with his modernizing rhetoric have left a mark or will evaporate together with their originator. More specifically, we may ask if Russia under Putin 2.0 will turn out to be a different place from that of Putin 1.0. Many of those who took part in the wave of open protests that followed in the wake of the rigged December 2011 Duma election certainly hoped and perhaps still believe so.

One of the most eloquent exponents of a belief in the possibility of change is Aleksei Navalnyi. Having emerged as a crusading young lawyer, he morphed from ubiquitous anti-corruption blogger to opposition leader and to a public relations nightmare for the Kremlin. His famed branding of United Russia, Putin's erstwhile "party of power," as a "party of crooks and thieves" quickly went viral and may have utterly destroyed the brand as such.[1] Navalnyi was arrested on December 5, the day after the Duma election. When subsequently released from a Moscow police station, he told a waiting crowd of supporters that, "We were arrested for 15 days in one country and released in another one."[2]

Cynics may smile and adopt a condescending attitude. They may admit that the uproar that followed in the wake of the election was real enough. It was novel, both in its reliance on social media, such as Twitter and Live Journal, and in bringing large sections of the country's urban elites into the streets. There can be little doubt that it did send shockwaves through the country's ruling elite. But can this really be construed as change, or even as a trigger for change, in any sense that would entail a revival of much-needed economic and political reform?

At a casual glance, the answer to this question will have to be negative. For all their fervent cyber activity and for all their loud claims that Putin must leave, the protesters in the end could not prevent him from winning a landslide first-round election victory. Although the initial wave of calls for honest elections did result in demotion and reassignment for Vladislav Surkov, the grey cardinal of the Kremlin, his creation of the brand and practice of "managed democracy" did prove its resilience.

Putin's return to the Kremlin may not have been accompanied by the anticipated fanfare. But it did provide yet another firm demonstration that supreme power in Russia will be undivided and unaccountable. With Medvedev humiliated, previously heated speculation over who was really in charge within the "tandem" came to an abrupt halt. Fearful of consequences for their own positions and for their associated revenue streams, members of the praetorian guards scrambled to adjust accordingly.

The bottom line is that predictability has returned. The next scheduled Duma election will not be held until 2016, and Vladimir Putin may be expected to remain as president at least until 2018. The prospects for a return any time soon to the path of radical reform that marked Putin's first term as president, in consequence, do not look good.

At the height of the rallies, members of the liberal opposition voiced hopes for early elections to a new Duma, which might re-energize the reform process. But it is hard to see how that can be arranged, within the rules of the constitution. The president does have a right to dissolve the Duma, but only in cases where his nominee for prime minister has been rejected three times by a majority of the deputies or where there has been a vote of no confidence in the government.[3] In either case, this would require Duma deputies to vote for an outcome where many presumably would lose their seats and associated perks. This does not seem very likely to occur. An alternative could be to simply invalidate the results of the December election. But since this would require admission by the president that widespread fraud had, indeed, taken place, it would seem to be even less likely. Assuming that all have been aware of these basic realities, the clamoring for early elections may be reduced to simple posturing and publicity seeking.

All of this is certainly true, and the tentative conclusions, as just mentioned, are not encouraging. A return to much-prized political stability may well turn out to entail stagnation, perhaps even to the point of fossilization, recalling the latter part of Leonid Brezhnev's rule. The reason why this must be taken so seriously derives from the fact that, in today's globalized economy, even standing still is tantamount to sinking.

A continued inflow of massive earnings from energy exports may keep the federal budget in order and Russia free of sovereign debt, but this constitutes little more than artificial life support. The sheer weight of evidence regarding what needs to be done in order to breathe new life into the Russian economy is simply overwhelming. If the price of oil should take another steep nosedive, then the consequences would be dire, indeed. The sharp decline that began in March 2012 provided a warning of what may come.

This said, we cannot ignore that something has snapped and that the regime will have to adapt. The immediate response by then President Medvedev to the initial outburst of anger from below was to announce that important political reform was in the making. Specific items on the list concerned legislation to facilitate registration of political parties and a return to direct elections of governors.[4] (These promises have since been acted upon, albeit with varying speed, determination, and dilution.) The question is what the implications of such changes in the formal rules of the game may be.

Will this turn out to have been no more than new twists in a familiar old game with predictable outcomes? Or, may it be construed as evidence that Putin 2.0 will, indeed, represent something qualitatively different from Putin 1.0? The Kremlin may certainly be suspected of being less than sincere in its proclaimed ambition to allow more political freedom. Yet the genie has now been let out of the bottle, and it may prove hard to get back in again. So, are we then looking at prospects for change that may be of consequence for the quality of governance and thus for the performance of the Russian economy?

This question goes to the very heart of what theories on institutional change are designed to capture, namely, the contrast between changes in formal rules and changes in informal norms. While the former may be achieved by direct agency, the latter will come about only indirectly, and the interplay is of core importance. Changes in values, beliefs, and expectations may trigger changes in the formal rules and be triggered by such changes. For a good outcome to occur, there must be mutual support and reinforcement. If rules are made that deviate too far from underlying norms, then a counter reaction will follow. The same will hold if values, beliefs, and expectations evolve away from existing systems of formal rules. It is against this analytical background that we shall proceed to look at the prospects for Russian economic development under Putin 2.0. The argument will be built in five consecutive steps.

The first will take a closer look at the Medvedev interlude, probing for changes in underlying systems of informal norms that may turn out to have lasting importance. More specifically, we shall look at responses to the nature and sudden termination of the ruling tandem, at the possible emergence of elements of civil society in Russia, and at effects of the high-profile campaign against corruption. This will set the stage for questioning the inherent stability of the regime.

The second step aims to show just how vulnerable the Russian economy is to swings in hydrocarbon prices. It will focus on how mounting fears of discontent from below have caused the Russian government to engage in lavish fiscal spending and, in consequence, to abstain from using the recent period of high energy export revenues to rebuild precautionary reserve funds. This will be shown to have aggravated the inherent vulnerability of the country's fiscal policy and foreign debt exposure to changes in energy prices.

The third step will approach the much-discussed question of imperative needs to undertake modernization of the Russian economy. It will outline why the challenge is so crucially important, discuss what it would take for a working solution to be found, and argue that, for all the huff and puff that emanated from the Medvedev Kremlin, the campaign in the end boiled down to little more than empty talk. This will provide important input for our concluding discussion on where the Russian economy may be headed.

The fourth step will argue that an important obstacle to change rests in the fact that the Russian economy has been made hostage to the fortunes of the energy complex. It will address the counterintuitive suggestion that resource-rich countries may be somehow "cursed" by those riches. It will show how the Putin regime has benefited both from an inflow of petrodollars, which has helped reduce debt and prop up the federal budget, and from being provided with an "energy weapon," which may be wielded in support of claims to regain respect as a great power.

The fifth and final step will expand on the negative impact that the energy riches have had on the Russian economy. This discussion will move beyond the academic debate on the possible presence of a "resource curse" and focus instead on how inherent institutional problems have combined to produce a form of "Russian curse," which is deeply rooted and rather distinctive. It will be seen to cast a long shadow over the prospects for serious reform to be implemented that may improve governance and thus promote both efficiency and much-needed modernization. Let us proceed now to look at the Medvedev interlude.

THE MEDVEDEV INTERLUDE

The main importance of the Medvedev presidency lies not so much in what was actually achieved, which was precious little, but rather in what was revealed. In retrospect, it may be tempting to conclude that it was all no more than a ruse. It was, arguably, a ploy devised by Putin to ensure that he could have his cake and eat it, too. Within the tandem, he could hold on to power while respecting the letter of the law, which prevented him from serving more than two consecutive terms as president. If we look simply at intentions, there would be an element of truth in this write-off. But if we turn to look also at consequences, matters are not so simple.

The cohabitation of two political leaders at the highest level of power at first seemed to belie the deeply-rooted belief that power in Russia must be undivided and unaccountable. The country was suddenly ruled by two men with very different agendas and personalities. It appeared for a time to be an open question as who was really in charge. Those who so preferred could pin their hopes on pending changes in the direction of increased legality, decreased corruption, a more cooperative foreign policy, and a more favorable investment climate. Others could look to Putin for reassurance that nothing much would change.

An important consequence of this deliberately introduced confusion was that widely different expectations were being formed. In some quarters, such expectations caused underlying liberal values and beliefs to be re-energized, in support of a hoped-for movement towards legality and accountability. It was the deep frustration of people who subsequently felt — justifiably so — that they had been simply deluded that triggered the protest movement against Putin. The chickens were, quite simply, coming home to roost.

By far the most important single lesson to be learned from the Medvedev interlude concerns how a political system in general approaches questions of succession at the top. The essence of a democratic system is that incumbents may face the prospect of loss of office without fear. The mantra of the transitology literature has been that we may speak of consolidated democracy only after elections that have brought peaceful and orderly changes in government. In Russia, none of this has much, if any, relevance. The potential consequences of being voted out of high office have remained dire, ranging from loss of income and assets, to prosecution and incarceration, or even worse. Problems concerning succession at the top have consequently not been taken lightly.

Towards the end of Boris Yeltsin's second term in office, health reasons alone made it clear that no amount of further manipulation could prolong his time in power. It also became obvious just how keen he was on finding a successor who could ensure his security. Having appointed and fired a number of prime ministers, who were deemed either to be too weak or not to be trusted, he finally settled on Putin. In keeping with the agreement, one of the latter's very first acts in power was to provide his benefactor with immunity against prosecution.[5]

As Putin's second term in power was, in turn, drawing to a close, considerations of security again came to the fore. Handing over the reins of power would be something of a gamble. There were distinct risks that new men in power might move to prosecute for alleged malfeasance during Putin's time in St. Petersburg.[6] There was also the question of his alleged personal fortune of maybe $40 billion, to which he has no formal (official) ownership title.[7] A successor would have to be strong enough to provide protection but also loyal enough not to get ambitious on his own account.

There were two leading candidates for the post of successor: Dmitry Medvedev and Sergei Ivanov. The former had served with Putin in St. Petersburg, had no power base of his own, and could be relied upon to remain loyal. The other was well connected within the power structures and could clearly be trusted to remain strong. But would he also be able to resist the temptation of usurping power for himself? Putin's choice of Medvedev turned out to be a good one. He did remain loyal, allowing his patron to ensure his own protection from behind the scenes.

The bottom line is that, during his first two terms in power, Putin was successful in ensuring that all such formal institutions that might have served to provide accountability in government were drained of all real content. By the time he opted to retreat into the tandem, power had been made entirely personal. He could, in consequence, hand over the keys to the Kremlin without running the risk of either prosecution or expropriation. There was, however, also a price to be paid.

What Putin had achieved may be usefully contrasted against what James Madison once wrote about political factions, in his perhaps most classic contribution to *The Federalist*: "There are two methods of curing the mischiefs of faction: the one, by removing its causes; the other, by controlling its effects." Noting that "liberty is to faction what air is to fire," Madison clearly rules out the former option. All men cannot be made the same, nor would it be wise to suppress their right to express different points of view. The solution was seen to lie in the creation of a republican form of government that allows factions to be organized and to compete within the framework of established constitutional rules.[8]

Turning to Russia under Putin, factional struggles during the 1990s had threatened to literally tear the state apart. But the solution when Putin assumed power was not seen to lie in working to improve institutions, whereby passions and interests might have been articulated and vetted against each other in an orderly manner. The essence of Putinism instead would be a *de facto* suppression of all such **formal** mechanisms whereby discontent may be channeled and whereby conflicts may find an open and orderly resolution. In the absence of such mechanisms, mounting pressures of discontent, which will build up in any type of political system, will have to find other outlets. Open street protests such as the mass rallies that began shaking Moscow towards the end of 2011 constitute the most visible illustration. But, as we shall argue here, the threat of a hostile takeover of power from within is of greater concern.

The second lesson to be drawn from the one-term Medvedev presidency concerns the associated question of the existence of civil society in Russia. By the time Medvedev moved into the Kremlin, conventional wisdom held that, during the first two terms of the Putin presidency, civil society had been simply beaten into submission. Subjects had been offered to engage in material self-enrichment, at the price of abstaining from any and all such forms of activity that are normally associated with a vibrant civil society.

During Medvedev's time in office, there were growing indications that some form of civil society might be returning to life. Yet, few, if any, were prepared for the mass mobilization that was to follow. The watershed arrived on September 24, 2011, when President Medvedev told a United Russia congress that he and Prime Minister Putin had agreed to simply swap jobs. Medvedev would step down, and Putin would run for the presidency. Accepting the nomination, Putin added insult to injury by saying that this was a decision the two had reached in 2007 but kept a secret.[9] The sheer arrogance of it all apparently was too much for many to stomach.

What made the ensuing wave of protests so difficult for the elite to "manage" was that this time, the protesters were neither pensioners nor other vulnerable groups complaining about hardship. Those who took to the streets were those that had stood to gain the most from the economic upturn under Putin. They were the winners, and they were not showing due gratitude. They were, on the contrary, making demands for public goods, such as honest elections, that the elite simply could not deliver. They conducted their protests in a peaceful, nonprovocative manner. They could not be appeased with additional fiscal spending. Ordering the riot police to beat the capital's cultural and entrepreneurial elite into pulp would have looked bad indeed.

The bewilderment of those in power was clearly manifested in Putin's initial reactions, which ranged from attempting to blame then U.S. Secretary of State Hilary Clinton for having inspired the protests, to denigrating the protesters as "Bandar-logs," the chattering monkey people in Rudyard Kipling's *Jungle Book*, whose incoherent behavior causes them to be scorned by the rest of the jungle.[10]

These reactions were quite in line with Putin's established way of badmouthing both foreign leaders and domestic opponents. But this time round, his demeanor was no longer viewed as a sign of strength. He was viewed instead as being utterly disconnected from reality. When Putin ran for re-election in 2004, his refusal to take part in public debates could be construed as the arrogance of power, of not condescending to even talk to his opponents. Now it was viewed as simple fear of having to answer pointed questions and perhaps even of being booed.[11]

It may certainly be argued that the Kremlin does not have any serious grounds for worry about the large protest rallies, or indeed about the vibrant activities that are taking place in various social media. There is little to indicate that Russia will experience rebellions from below that are similar in kind to the famed "Arab Spring" or even to the "color revolutions" that transformed Georgia in 2003 and Ukraine in 2004. As mentioned, the real cause for concern lies in a different direction: in a threat that emerges from within the elite.

In a comment on his own role as officially approved presidential candidate, billionaire Mikhail

Prokhorov claimed that he abhorred the prospect of a revolution from below and remained hopeful that divisions within the elite would force the regime to accommodate at least some demands for reform: "I think that the liberal part of the elite is bigger and bigger from day to day, because I have a lot of calls from different levels, and they really express their support for my candidacy."[12]

The importance of this observation lies in the fact that there may, indeed, be support from within the elite for proceeding with cautious reform. Some, like Russian political commentator Stanislav Belkovsky, have even suggested the advent of a second "perestroika."[13] The presumed reasons vary. Some may have developed genuine sympathies for the need to reform. Others may view reform as a simple necessity to avoid being swept away by a tidal wave of discontent from below. The bottom line is that formal changes in the rules may be expected. The challenge to the regime will be similar to that encountered during Putin's first term as president: to allow some formal changes in the rules of the game to proceed while ensuring that such changes will not in any fundamental way alter the game as such.

The third, and by far the most striking, lesson to be drawn from the Medvedev interlude is a direct corollary of the president's ambition to appear as a champion of legality. By projecting an image of himself as a crusader against corruption, he provided an implicit carte blanche from the very top for striking revelations. With the president taking the lead in castigating corruption, hard line officials were unable to crack down against people like Aleksei Navalnyi, who made a name for himself as a fearless anti-corruption blogger. Nor was it possible to prevent other members of officialdom from speaking out of school. On the contrary, doing so may even have been perceived by some as a sign of loyalty. Under a different president, one would, for example, not have expected to hear Russia's top military prosecutor, Sergei Fridinsky, tell the *Rossiyskaya Gazeta* that at least 20 percent of the defense budget is being siphoned off every year via various forms of fraud.[14]

The main importance of these revelations lies not so much in the revelations as such, as in what they say about the political system that Putin has built. His regime has often been accused of being authoritarian, and parallels have been drawn both to the Soviet order and to the autocracy of the Russian imperial order. This is at least partly misleading. It is true that the Kremlin does project an authoritarian image and that there have been cases of conduct that recall memories out of Russia's dark past. One need only mention here the destruction of Yukos; the kangaroo trials against its Chief Executive Officer Mikhail Khodorkovsky; the spate of unresolved killings of journalists, notably but not exclusively Anna Politkovskaya; and the beating to death in a prison cell of the promising young lawyer, Sergei Magnitsky.

Yet, if Putin's regime had, indeed, been truly authoritarian, it would have had little trouble dealing with at least the most egregious forms of self-enrichment and diversion of funds that are so clearly detrimental to the interests of the state. To be specific, it is hard to see how an authoritarian agenda of rearmament and force projection can be made to agree, with allowing a fifth and possibly more of the defense budget to be simply stolen every year.

There has to be a reason, and that reason, we shall argue, goes to the very heart of the political order of

Putinism. Assuming that the Kremlin remains in firm control of the security services, it should have little problem tracking down the main culprits that have been robbing the state blind. It is, indeed, very likely that extensive documentation has already been collected. But no serious action is taken, and for good reason. Allowing members of the elite to tap into the resources of the state and to move the loot into safe havens abroad has become the linchpin of the implicit contract between the ruler and his boyars. Cracking down might trigger a veritable civil war within and among the elites, and, in the end, perhaps even a hostile takeover of power.

We shall have reason to return to the systemic implications of these observations in our concluding discussion on the prospects for reform. Here we shall proceed to look at how Russia was affected by and emerged out of the global financial crisis. This is done in order to emphasize the crucial role of hydrocarbon prices and the inherent weakness of the nonenergy sectors of the Russian economy.

GLOBAL FINANCIAL CRISIS

The global financial crisis struck Russia hard, albeit with some delay. During the fall of 2008, when the subprime mortgage crisis was sending shock waves through the global economy, Russia remained outwardly unperturbed. It was held, or at least pretended, that the crisis was U.S.-made and would have little impact on Russia. As late as at the World Economic Forum in Davos in early 2009, Minister of Finance Alexei Kudrin could still famously claim that Russia was "an island of stability."[15] Reality, however, was about to catch up.

Over the first two terms of the Putin presidency, the Russian economy had grown by on average 7 percent per annum, and the federal budget had been kept solidly in the black. In 2008, Russian gross domestic product (GDP) was still growing at 5.2 percent, and the federal budget still turned in a surplus, corresponding to 4.1 percent of GDP. In 2009, Russian GDP contracted by 7.9 percent, and the federal budget recorded a deficit corresponding to 5.9 percent of GDP.[16] The drastic nature of this transformation calls for three important observations to be made.

The first brings home just how prudent the Russian government had been in accumulating precautionary reserves while the going was still good. Central Bank foreign currency reserves peaked on August 8, 2008, at $598.1 billion; and on September 1, the "rainy day" Reserve Fund reached its peak of $142.6 billion.[17] When the budget swung into deficit and when calls were made on the Central Bank to provide crisis support, there was ample room for such intervention.

The second observation concerns how the crisis measures were formulated. There is broad consensus that the government implemented an anti-crisis program which, in the words of Pekka Sutela, "rightly earned accolades" from several international organizations: one "has to agree with the IMF [International Monetary Fund] and the World Bank's assessment now that Russia's anti-crisis policy was a major success overall: timely, consistent, and effective."[18] Closer inspection, however, will reveal that the authorities placed a heavy premium on measures that were clearly designed to preserve systemic stability. The main priority was to bail out the country's highly leveraged oligarchs. This was done by the government, offering an immediate credit line allowing debts coming due to foreign banks to be paid. It was done by the Central Bank, spending about $100 billion of its reserves on market interventions to ensure a gradual devaluation of the ruble. While the first move offered well-connected oligarchs to escape immediate margin calls, which might have pushed them into bankruptcy, the latter offered them ample time to convert rubles into dollars at favorable rates of exchange.

As Sutela puts it, the latter was tantamount to a *de facto* privatization of a good part of the nation's foreign currency reserves.[19] It was, however, also quite consistent with what Clifford Gaddy and Barry Ickes have presented as Putin's "protection racket."[20] While the going was good, the oligarchs acted as loyal clients of Putin. When they fell on hard times, the patron had to live up to his part of the bargain, which was to offer protection. Although there was blatant favoritism involved, it cannot be denied that by saving banks and oligarchs, the regime also prevented a slide into mass unemployment and possible social unrest.

Our third, and by far most important, observation concerns the impact of the crisis on Russian prestige. During Yeltsin's time in power, the Kremlin was becoming ever more insistent that Russia must be granted access to all those international "clubs" where other great powers regularly meet. A case in point was the G7 group of leading industrialized nations.[21] Although Russia was far, indeed, from qualifying for membership on its economic merits, political considerations caused the others to occasionally grant Russia informal membership in an expanded G8.[22] In effect, it meant that Russian delegates were welcome at cocktails and photo ops but not at closed discussions on matters of global economic policy.

At the outset of the first Putin presidency, there emerged another, and to the Russian elite, far more palatable frame of reference: the BRICs. Introduced by Goldman Sachs analyst Jim O'Neill in 2001, this catchy acronym denoted a group of fast-growing economies that included Brazil, Russia, India, and China. At their first formal summit meeting, held in the Russian city of Yekaterinburg on June 16, 2009, the leaders of the four BRIC economies had much to say about the importance of their group as a whole, as an emerging challenge to the established world economic order, and about their prospects to take a joint lead in achieving global economic recovery.

Remaining within the world of finance, it was striking to note how quickly Russia's financial markets rebounded. Investors could derive pleasure from the fact that, over 2009, the Russian Trading System (RTS) index of the Moscow Stock Exchange rose from 632 to 1,445, with market capitalization rising from $55.3 to $146.7 billion. The rise would continue over 2010, albeit at a slower pace, with the index ending the year at 1,770 and market capitalization at $186.6 billion.[23]

Having looked set for extinction "as a class" in 2009, in 2010, Russia's famed oligarchs would be back in the game. Or, at least most of them would. According to Forbes, in 2010, the number of Russian billionaires had risen to 62 from merely 32 in 2009, and their joint worth had more than doubled, from $142 billion to $297 billion.[24] The market rebound was clearly driven by a rapid rise in the price of oil. Over 2009, the price of Urals crude, which is Russia's main export blend, increased from $34.20 to $72.08 per barrel, and it continued climbing in 2010, ending the year at $90.94 per barrel.[25] The immediate impact was felt on the current account, where hydrocarbon revenues are of paramount importance in generating a much-needed surplus. Having dropped from $103.5 billion in 2008 to a mere $48.6 billion in 2009, the surplus rose to $70.6 billion in 2010.[26] Given that every $1 change in the price per barrel is generally estimated to translate into a change of about $2 billion in federal budget revenue, the rebound also had a profound impact on federal budget performance.

All told, we may conclude that what rode to the rescue for the Russian economy was a broad recovery on global energy markets. The surprising speed of the turnaround would be reflected also in a drastic transformation of Russian moods, from a deep sense of crisis in the midst of 2009 to renewed complacency by the end of 2010. It may be useful to recollect just how deep it was believed at the time that Russia would sink.

During the first half of 2009, the Reserve Fund was being depleted at such a rate that in April, Finance Minister Kudrin predicted that it would be "practically exhausted" in 2010.[27] By the end of July, the government announced that it was expecting federal budget deficits corresponding to 9.4 percent of GDP for 2009, to 7.5 percent for 2010, and to 4.3 percent for 2011.[28] In order to cover the shortfall, sales of Eurobonds of up to $20 billion was envisioned for 2010 alone, and more was expected to follow.[29]

As it turned out, the budget deficit for 2009 stopped at 5.9 percent of GDP. For 2010, the number was kept to 4.1 percent, and the federal budget actually ended with a surplus of 0.8 percent for 2011.[30] In tandem with this improvement in budget performance, reserves also stabilized and began rising again. From a low point of $383.8 billion at the end of April 2009, by the end of August 2011, Central Bank reserves had reached $545.0 billion, closing in on the record high of $598.1 billion that was achieved on August 8, 2008. The number has since remained at or slightly above $500 billion.[31] The Reserve Fund, meanwhile, continued to shrink, but at an orderly pace, from $60.5 billion at the outset of 2010, to $25.4 billion at the outset of 2011. In February 2012, a large one-time deposit out of 2011 energy earnings caused it to rise again, to $61.4 billion.[32] As the crisis in the euro zone deepened, the world of finance came up with another suggestive acronym: PIIGS, denoting the crisis-ridden euro economies of Portugal, Ireland, Italy, Greece, and Spain. If compared to the members of this sordid group, Russia looked positively inspiring. With a debt-to-GDP ratio of less than 10 percent, Russia looked good, even if compared to the northern group of less crisis-ridden European Union (EU) member states.

Following the downgrade of U.S. sovereign debt in August 2011, which was triggered by congressional gridlock over the debt ceiling, it was even becoming questionable how much longer the EU and the United States would remain as global economic leaders and role models. It was surely tempting to join O'Neill in wondering how long it would take investors to "accept that the growth markets are actually fiscally more prudent and financially in better shape than in the Western world."[33]

If, however, Russia were to be compared to the other members of what is now known as the BRICS following the April 2011 inclusion into the group of South Africa, then a completely different picture emerges. During 2009, the main year of the crisis, both China and India maintained solid growth, with GDP increasing by, respectively, 9.1 and 5.7 percent, and Brazil just barely managed to hold the line, with a drop of merely 0.2 percent.[34] In a provocative commentary, Dmitry Trenin concluded that:

Moscow ought to forget about trying to undermine America's global hegemony and concentrate instead on retaining its place in the 'top league' of world powers. China, India, and Brazil are candidates for membership in it. Russia is a candidate for exit.[35]

In a speech at a Global Policy Forum in the Russian city Yaroslavl in early September 2011, economist Paul Krugman, winner of the 2008 Nobel Prize in economics, had even harsher words to offer: "Russia really doesn't belong in the group. It's a petro-economy in terms of world trade." While Krugman notes that Russia does have potential to **become** a part of the group, at the moment it is not even close. India and China come across as labor-abundant, rapid-growth economies, and although Brazil relies on raw-materials oriented exports, it does have a strong manufacturing sector: "Russia doesn't fit at all."[36]

Keeping in mind Krugman's observation that Russia does at least have the potential to become a high-growth economy based on drivers other than energy exports, let us proceed now to look at how that potential has been mismanaged, at how empty talk of modernization has come to serve as a substitute for serious action.

EMPTY TALK OF MODERNIZATION

Looking beyond financial markets and macroeconomic stabilization, we may ask what lessons the Russian leadership was ready and able to learn from the financial crisis. Did it absorb the implications of depending so heavily on the global market for hydrocarbons? Did it realize the imperative need to diversify away from this dependence and to build precautionary reserves while the flow of petrodollars remained high? Or, was it, on the contrary, bent on simply digging in, on reaping the benefits while possible and deferring any type of change that might threaten systemic stability? The latter would very clearly turn out to be the case, much to the detriment of the future development of the Russian economy and of Russian society at large.

The main challenge to Russian economic policymaking surely remains that of securing global economic competitiveness. Given the tremendous brain power that was housed in the old Soviet "military industrial complex" and the fact that Russia on the whole has a highly skilled and educated work force, it is rather sad to note that the country presently has an almost zero presence on global high-tech markets. The contrast against China and India in this regard is highly sobering.[37]

There can be little question that those in power are well aware of the problem. While there has been considerable complacency about swings in capital flows, the very real risk of being relegated to the rather ignominious status as a mere raw materials appendix to the developed nations, notably including China, has been taken very seriously. The need to modernize was, in consequence, to become something of a mantra or a hallmark of the Medvedev presidency.

In a much cited article titled "Go, Russia!" published in September 2009, President Medvedev was quite frank: "Should a primitive economy based on raw materials and endemic corruption accompany us into the future?" Making his case for the need to modernize, he spoke about a "humiliating dependence on raw materials," about how "finished goods produced in Russia are largely plagued by their extremely low competitiveness," and about the need to stamp out "bribery, theft, intellectual and spiritual laziness, and drunkenness."[38]

It was a powerful statement, which did inspire hope for serious action to follow. There also did seem to be an awareness of what would need to be done. In a major speech just before he was elected president, Medvedev had outlined what would become the main priorities of his presidency. Advancing a long list of priorities, he emphasized that the road to modernity must be paved with the "four I's" of innovation, institutions, infrastructure, and investment.[39] If we ignore for the moment the rather obvious need to upgrade the country's seriously dilapidated infrastructure, the key to understanding Russia's future may be seen to lie in the interplay between the remaining three.

At the face of it, it may all seem so very simple. Good institutions will promote increased investment, which in turn will promote innovation and global integration. But the chain works equally well in the opposite direction: bad institutions will depress investment which in turn will hamper innovation and lead to isolation. The question of modernization must be viewed against precisely this background. It is not sufficient that Russia has come to **look** like a modern society. It is true that the townscapes of major cities like Moscow and St. Petersburg are presently very similar to those of other big cities around the world. The sheer density of very up-market shopping gallerias may be as high as in any other big metropolis. But this is all largely deceptive.

The core question concerns how decisions are made **behind** the modern façades. Are decisionmakers confident that legal and economic institutions are of sufficient quality to ensure that investment will yield adequate return? Do they feel safe from predation by interests protected by the government, or indeed by the government itself? If we look at how little is being achieved despite the massive inflow of revenues from hydrocarbon exports, the answer to the latter questions must be firmly negative.

For lack of a better measure, we shall argue that the share of fixed capital investment in GDP constitutes a good predictor of the prospects for future growth and technological change. According to World Bank numbers for 2010, that share was 45 percent (and rising) for China and 22 percent (stagnant) for Russia.[40] If, moreover, we were to take into account that investment goods in the Russian economy are predominantly bought from monopoly producers charging inflated prices, the share of investment in Russian GDP, measured at world market prices, would drop to below 10 percent.[41] The reasons are as simple as they are troublesome.

In the context of an economy where contracts and property rights are shaky at best, where government is unaccountable and prone to discretionary imposition of what Clifford Gaddy and Barry Ickes have referred to as "informal taxes,"[42] and where members of the bureaucracy are always on the prowl for extortionary bribes, the rational strategy will be one of short-term spot-market trading and of ensuring that profits and capital flows are kept well below the radar screens of predatory government agencies. In addition to depressing the overall level of fixed capital investment, this environment will also give rise to what has come to be known as "round tripping," i.e., that a substantial share of capital flowing into and out of Russia is made up of Russian capital leaving and returning, following a brief stay in some foreign account.

The importance of this latter phenomenon may be reflected in the fact that Cyprus tends to be among the top foreign investors in the Russian economy.[43] It is also significant that single events of a mainly political nature have left big marks in the charts, such as when Rosneft and Gazprom purchased Yukos assets in the first half of 2007 by allegedly securing foreign credits of, respectively, $25.1 billion and $5.8 billion.[44] Much of the heavy inflow of capital that was recorded in 2007 could also be explained by Gazprom Netherlands investing to buy out Shell from Sakhalin. From a perspective of modernization and global integration, the latter should probably be counted with a negative sign.

The reason why all of this is so important rests in highlighting the bogus nature of capital flows to and from Russia. Given that "round tripping" capital will be logged as capital flight on departure and as foreign direct investment (FDI) on arrival, it follows that both these flows will be greatly inflated in importance. While the numbers as such may be correct, they will generate a warped understanding of Russia's integration into the global economy. What the Russian economy so desperately needs is technology and management skills that may promote serious modernization. The hallmark of "true" FDI is that it embodies precisely these contributions. Returning Russian money does not.

Numerous reasons may be advanced to explain why Russian actors engage in the practice of "round tripping." Ranging from tax evasion to money laundering and to outright criminal activity, they all have one feature in common: investors prefer to keep their activities out of sight of potential predators. This may be taken as firm evidence in support of the general understanding that the "climate" for productive investment in the Russian economy has come to be so widely perceived as being simply appalling.

Financial market analysts have routinely advanced numbers on what the capitalization of the Moscow Stock Exchange **would** have been if Russia had been judged on its purely economic merits. An excellent illustration is that of Gazprom. In 2000, it had a market value of $13.8 billion, which was tiny compared to ExxonMobil ($299 billion), Shell ($121 billion) or even Texaco ($38 billion). In a suggestive comparison from the time by Bill Browder of Hermitage Capital Management, if Gazprom had been optimistically valued at the same level as Exxon per barrel of hydrocarbon reserves, it would have been worth $1.8 trillion, or 132 times the current market price. The government's stake would then have been worth $698 billion, or 4.6 times the entire Russian national debt.[45]

In addition to the discount applied by markets to Russian stock, simply because it is Russian, we may add that the role of the stock market in the Russian economy has been set in decline. In the run-up to the 2012 presidential election, Dmitry Pankin, head of the Federal Service for Financial Markets, bemoaned the poverty of financial markets in Russia. The market capitalization of the stock market, which used to be 100 percent of GDP, had fallen to less than 50 percent of GDP. Domestic initial public offerings in 2010 were minuscule at 0.1 percent of GDP, and the volume of corporate bonds was extremely small, amounting to only 6 percent of GDP. Mutual funds, which are so important in mature economies, barely existed at 0.3 percent of GDP. The causes of this dearth of financial markets are, according to Pankin, to be found in poor law enforcement and judicial services. His verdict is not a happy one: "The road to render Moscow a financial center is very long."[46]

What makes it so hard to inspire confidence in investors is that the Russian government routinely engages in forms of behavior that cause investors to demand a very large discount. Although admittedly extreme, the campaign to destroy Yukos Oil has often been advanced as an illustration of the price that Russia is forced to pay for the behavior of its government. A more recent illustration of the same concerns the tragic case of Sergei Magnitsky, a promising young Russian lawyer who was employed by Browder's Hermitage Investment fund. In November 2009, he was battered to death in police custody. His gruesome fate has become an international issue of major proportions, and his friends, led by Browder, have even succeeded in persuading President Barack Obama to impose restrictions on a number of officials implicated in his death.[47] At the 2012 World Economic Forum in Davos, Browder took the opportunity to ask why the guilty parties were not being prosecuted.

In the pointed words of journalist Gideon Rachman, blogging from the event for the *Financial Times*, the response from Russian Deputy Prime Minister Igor Shuvalov was (presumably) meant to sound reasonable and reassuring: "He described the case as 'horrendous' and said that some people had already lost their jobs and been charged over it." But it was very difficult to get to the bottom of the case, "because the 'system' was protecting some guilty people." The clear implication was that nothing would happen. Most importantly, Rachman reports having been told by one participant that based on Shuvalov's answer alone, he had decided not to proceed with a big potential investment in Russia.[48] It was somehow symptomatic of this general atmosphere of "untouchables" that, towards the end of 2010, while Judge Victor Danilikin was busy reading the 250-page verdict in the second "kangaroo" trial of Mikhail Khodorkovsky, Medvedev was addressing a business council on modernization, bemoaning the fact that so few Russian companies had opted to issue equity during the year: "Part of the problem, of course, is our investment climate, which is bad. Very bad."[49]

The only tangible measure that was taken during Medvedev's time in the Kremlin, in an effort to make up for Russia's lagging position in the sphere of global high-tech development, was the creation of a technopark in the Moscow region town of Skolkovo. Designed to become a Russian version of the American Silicon Valley, the hype around this project has been intense. Substantial efforts have been made to attract companies, foreign as well as domestic, and many have responded, at least in name. President Medvedev also made a point of being filmed visiting the real Silicon Valley, where he could tout his new iPad and meet all those brilliant young Russians who prefer to pursue their ventures outside Russia.

For all its rhetorical efforts, it remains questionable if the Russian regime is capable of understanding that the real Silicon Valley is not about geography. It is about a state of mind, one, moreover, that is anathema to everything that Putinism has stood for. Talented young Russians are responding to this realization by voting with their feet. According to numbers released by the Federal Audit Chamber in February 2011, about 1.25 million Russians, many of whom likely were young entrepreneurs, had emigrated over the past 3 years.[50]

An oft-cited case in point is that of Andre Geim, a brilliant young Russian-born scientist, now residing in Manchester, England, with a Dutch passport. Following the announcement that he and his collaborator Konstantin Novoselov had won the Nobel Prize in Physics for 2010, it was immediately announced that the two would be invited by the Skolkovo leadership to join the venture. This was an offer they had little problem refusing, claiming that:

> the Kremlin could throw money at science, but research would still be stymied by corruption, red tape and a lack of the vital international teams and facilities needed to engage in groundbreaking work.

When asked specifically by a Russian journalist what it would take for him to return, Geim responded curtly: "Reincarnation."[51]

Let us turn now to the core question of how it can be that a country that is simply awash in theoretically investable funds, and that has such an impressive pool of talent to draw on, succeeds in achieving so little. The first part of the answer calls for a closer look at the source of the financial wealth, i.e., the country's energy complex.

HOSTAGE TO THE ENERGY COMPLEX

The rise to power of Putin was intimately intertwined with a spectacular rise in income from hydrocarbon exports. In the wake of the meltdown on the country's financial markets in August 1998, the prevailing sentiment was doom and gloom. Most of 1999 was marked by expectations that it would take a very long time for Russia to recover. But behind the scenes, a powerful recovery was under way. A massive devaluation of the ruble had caused imports to plummet, making room for domestic producers with spare capacity to respond rapidly. During the second half of 1999, the Russian economy was already expanding at double digits.[52]

When Putin moved into the Kremlin following his landslide election victory in March 2000, the general sentiments about the Russian economy remained grim. Then the hydrocarbon cavalry rode to the rescue, helping boost the image of Putin as an efficient economic manager. The price of Urals crude had bottomed at $8.73 per barrel on December 4, 1998. When Yeltsin resigned at the end of 1999, it was still at $24.71. By the time of Medvedev's inauguration in May 2008, it had risen to $120.01.[53] It was still a couple of months shy of its peak. The spike in the price of oil, moreover, was only part of the story. Putin's image was further enhanced by the fact that both prices and volumes were rising in tandem, which is unusual indeed.

Due to the general dislocation of the 1990s, Russian oil production had slumped from a high of 11.48 million barrels per day (bpd) in 1987 to an annual average of around 6 million bpd. In 2000, it was still at no more than 6.54 million bpd. Then output began to climb, driven by improved efficiency in operations by the privatized Russian oil companies. Much was for short-term gain, "creaming" reservoirs that had been neglected during the Yeltsin era. But it did bring a rise in output. By 2008, when Putin moved out of the Kremlin, Russian oil production had risen by more than half, to 9.88 million bpd.[54] In the latter year, Russia was tied with Saudi Arabia for the role as the largest producer of oil in the world.

It was the combination of these two trends that drove the transformation of the Russian economy. As outlined previously, it generated a huge current account surplus, allowed foreign debt to be almost eliminated, and made room for precautionary reserves to be built within the federal budget. By the time the global financial crisis struck, Russia had a most inspiring track record of successful fiscal conservatism. But the hydrocarbon bonanza also had a dark side, one that would taint the image of Russia as a reliable partner.

As the Russian energy complex began rising in prominence, accounting for about two-thirds of exports and half of federal budget revenue, the Kremlin found that it could be of use not only in achieving macroeconomic stability. The export of gas in particular offered the opportunity of wielding an "energy weapon." At the outset of Putin's presidency, Russia was generally viewed as an economic basket case and as politically irrelevant. As the energy riches caused Russian confidence to rise, foreign imagery was also being transformed. Pictures of an emerging "energy superpower" were projected.[55] Harkening back to the days of Ronald Reagan and the Cold War, warnings were again issued to European nations about the dangers inherent in becoming reliant on Russian gas.[56] Even the specter of a resumption of the Cold War itself was brought back.[57]

Barring the Cold War rhetoric, which is so wide of the mark as to be simply ludicrous, there were serious grounds for worry. The reasons related mainly, if not exclusively, to Russian pipeline policy and to the export of gas. Oil has been important to Russia as a revenue source, but oil is fungible. It can be transported in many different ways, and it can be bought and sold on spot markets around the world. As amply evidenced by the flamboyant but essentially empty rhetoric of Venezuelan President Hugo Chavez, threats of ceasing oil deliveries carry little weight unless backed by a large cartel.

Gas is very different. To the extent that gas is transported via pipeline, which has long been the predominant mode, the two sides will be locked into mutual dependence, and there can be no serious talk of a global market for gas. The arrival of liquid natural gas (LNG) and shale gas is transforming this picture, but it has had very little impact on Russian policymaking to date. Close to 100 percent of Russian export of gas goes to Europe and to neighboring Commonwealth of Independent States (CIS), and it is all via pipeline. There is some gas being exported from Sakhalin as LNG, but, for the present purpose, it may be safely ignored. The evolution of Russian gas export policy during the first two terms of the Putin presidency was marked by three important features, all of which gave rise to serious conflict.

The first concern is that undertaking a transition from central economic planning to market economy entailed a drastic break with the old practice of heavily subsidized prices on domestic energy consumption. For political reasons, the Russian government made sure that harmonizing domestic gas prices would proceed slowly—so slowly, in fact, that the process still remains to be completed. For national gas giant Gazprom, this implied that losses on the domestic market had to be compensated via profits on foreign markets. It offered a great deal of leeway in discriminating between different foreign customers. While countries that were deemed as friendly to the Kremlin would see their prices rise slowly, those considered less friendly could be slapped with drastic increases. Conflicts over such price hikes could also be laced with supply shut-offs, all of which combined to give the Kremlin an image as an energy bully.

The **second** and equally contentious area of conflict derives from the fact that Russia inherited a gas pipeline infrastructure that transports gas to Europe across territories that are now independent states, mainly Ukraine and Belarus. As Gazprom got locked into pricing conflicts with such transit states, it rapidly discovered that its own highly lucrative export to the EU could be held hostage. Deliveries of gas to Ukraine could, for example, not be shut down without also shutting down deliveries to EU member states. The conclusion that the transit states must be sidelined was done by building bypass pipelines such as the Nord Stream, which already transports gas directly from Vyborg in Russia to Greifswald in Germany, and the South Stream, which is to transport gas from the Caspian Basin via the Black Sea to south-eastern Europe. Both Poland and the Baltic states responded vehemently to what they viewed as a project designed to shut down their energy supplies without disrupting the flow to Germany.

The third and potentially most serious area of conflict is a form of collateral damage. When pricing conflicts between Gazprom and Ukraine led to major supply shutoffs in 2006 and again in 2009, several EU member states found that their supplies were also shut off, causing them to freeze in the dead of winter. Although ambitions were not to take sides on who was mainly to blame, Moscow or Kiev, it was inevitable that the reputation of Gazprom, and by implication that of the Kremlin, as a reliable partner and supplier suffered a great deal of damage. This fed into ongoing

European ambitions to formulate a common energy policy based on competition and diversification of the sources of EU energy imports. The "third energy package" introduced explicit demands for ownership "unbundling," i.e., that Gazprom must divest itself of its pipeline assets.

As Russia began to profit from the rapid increase in earnings from hydrocarbon exports, another and more academically slanted issue came to the fore: "Dutch disease" or a possible "resource curse." The "Dutch disease" is a standard term in economics, once coined by *The Economist* to describe the consequences for the Dutch economy of opening up the Groeningen gas field in the North Sea. In short, it says that a rapid rise in commodity exports causes upward pressure on the exchange rate, which in turn stimulates imports and makes life harder for noncommodity exporters. As domestic resources are drawn into the commodity sector, other sectors suffer compounded damage, and the final outcome will be a seriously warped economic structure. The Netherlands in the end did not fall prey to this disease, nor are there any signs that Russia has suffered more than mild symptoms of the same.

A more complex set of consequences of the broader "resource curse" hold that economies with a dominant resource sector will tend to be less democratic and will suffer lower rates of growth than more diversified economies. The latter are features that we shall return to, in a qualified form, in our concluding discussion. First, however, we shall round off the portrayal of Moscow as hostage to its own energy complex by looking at the question of sustainability. Again, this shall be focused more on gas than on oil.

As the Russian economy emerged out of the global financial crisis, the reasons why gas is so important were made plain. It is true that recovery was greatly assisted by a rise in the price of oil. The annual average price of Urals crude, received from non-CIS states, peaked at $95.27 in 2008. During the crisis year 2009, it dropped by 40 percent to $57.47. It then began to rise to $76.24 in 2010 and $107.30 in 2011.[58] With some delay, this also fed into rising prices for gas.

The problem for Moscow is that relying on a steady growth in prices will be fraught with danger. There will come a point where the price grows so high that it triggers another global recession, the implication of which would be another massive "correction" for Russia. Sustainability must be sought in increased output and in making more room for export by promoting domestic energy efficiency. Neither presently offers much inspiration.

The Russian oil sector is stagnating, and its reserves are being depleted. Its glory days were associated with the discovery of a number of supergiant fields in Western Siberia, such as the Samotlor, all of which have long since passed their peak. It is true that the post-crisis years have seen further expansion in Russian oil production. In 2009, it rose to 10.04 million bpd. This allowed Russia to actually bypass Saudi Arabia, which had cut back its production from 10.84 to 9.89 million bpd. But in 2010 and 2011, Russian production leveled off at about 10.3 million bpd.[59]

The substantial additions to output that were recorded during Putin's first two terms were chiefly due to better management of existing fields. That low hanging fruit has now been plucked, and exploration for new fields will take place in less accessible and geologically less favorable areas. When announcements are made of new record levels having been reached, the added volumes are measured not in millions, but rather in tens of thousands of bpd.

At the end of 2009, the total proven reserves of oil in the Russian Federation were 74.2 billion barrels, or 5.6 percent of the global total. The reserves-to-production ratio, which defines the number of years the remaining reserves will last at current levels of production, was no more than 20.3 years. In comparison, the total proven reserves for Saudi Arabia stood at 264.6 billion barrels, and its reserves-to-production ratio was 74.6 years.[60] The much publicized fact that Russia has overtaken Saudi Arabia as the largest producer in the world must be viewed against this background.

Natural gas offers a completely different and potentially more inspiring picture. At the end of 2009, Russia had proven reserves of 44.38 trillion cubic meters (tcm), or 23.7 percent of the global total. Its reserves-to-production ratio was 84.1 years. Iran and Qatar, by contrast, had proven reserves of, respectively, 29.61 tcm and 25.37 tcm. Russian production of natural gas also far outstripped that of its rivals. In 2009, Russia produced 527.5 billion cubic meters (bcm). Iran was second, at 131.2 bcm, and Qatar was third, at 89.3 bcm.[61]

The problem here is that despite, or perhaps due to, its dominant position, Gazprom has not been managing its reserves very well. Its output over the past decade has been essentially flat. In 2001, it produced 512.0 bcm of gas (excluding gas condensate). In 2006, output had risen to 556.0 bcm; but during the crisis year 2009, it fell back to 461.5 bcm. In 2010, it recovered to 508.6 bcm.[62] Estimates for 2011 show a further rise to 513.2 bcm, which is about the same as in 2001.[63]

Part of the reason is that Gazprom has an equally poor track record in exploration. It has long depended on a handful of supergiant fields in Western Siberia, all of which have long since passed their peak. It has also been slow in developing existing finds, such as the giant offshore Shtokman field and the Kovytka field in Eastern Siberia that it wrested from TNK-BP in 2007 and then placed on hold. Pressure from the Kremlin has caused the company to step up its exploration efforts, and 2011 saw a record 686.4 bcm gas reserve increment.[64] But there is much past neglect to make up.

Gazprom's legal monopoly on exports, and its control over the country's huge "Unified Gas Supply System," has also been holding back more efficient independent producers such as Itera and Novatek. Again, pressure from the Kremlin is forcing change. Gazprom was slapped with a major tax increase in 2011, and parts of its assets have been taken over by the independents. The hands of "friends of Putin" have clearly been at work behind the scenes.[65]

But by far the greatest challenge both to Gazprom and to Russia is the arrival of "unconventional gas," notably shale gas, which has caused a complete change of scenes. In November 2011, the International Energy Association (IEA) prophesied that we may now be entering a "Golden Age of Gas." Under this scenario, gas demand grows by 2 percent a year between 2009 and 2035. Even in a less upbeat scenario, the IEA sees annual gas demand rise by 1.7 percent, or by 55 percent for the period as a whole.[66] In its latest Energy Outlook, BP similarly anticipates that by 2030, gas may have come to rival coal and oil as a primary energy source.[67] Since gas is cleaner than other fossil fuels, this is positive news for the environment, and it should be positive news for Moscow. But is this really the case?

At the end of 2009, the United States had no more than 6.93 trillion centimeters (cm) in proven reserves of natural gas. But in that same year, it still bypassed Russia to become the largest gas producer in the world, with an output of 593.4 bcm.[68] While Moscow could delight in having replaced Saudi Arabia as the largest oil producer in the world, it had to accept being bypassed by the United States as the largest gas producer in the world. In 2010, U.S. output rose further, to reach 611 bcm, compared to 589.9 bcm for Russia.[69]

Both Gazprom and the Kremlin are poorly positioned to respond to this new challenge. The Russian understanding of energy security has long been marked by a perceived need to control energy flows and to lock in its customers. This has generated an obsession with pipeline construction, to the detriment of investment in LNG. Russia's first terminal for LNG was built by Shell on Sakhalin and came on line in 2009. It was long thought that the supergiant Shtokman field had been earmarked for LNG, to be transported to the United States. But now Gazprom has wrested control over Sakhalin from Shell, and Shtokman no longer is destined for LNG.

Gazprom may have thought that LNG could be safely ignored. It is expensive and does not offer control to the extent that pipelines do. The shale gas revolution, or simply the "shale gale," changed all that. Following years of massive investment by Qatar, in particular in export terminals for LNG, and by the United States in import terminals for the same, the United States suddenly was no longer in need of imported gas. With its import terminals standing idle, LNG was instead rerouted to Europe, where a gas glut emerged. Gazprom suffered doubly, both from a loss of market shares to the cheaper LNG and from having to agree to demands from its customers that oil-price linkage must give way to spot-market pricing.

Although the Kremlin remains obsessed with building pipelines, the wisdom of this policy is coming under serious doubt. Its aggressive pipeline diplomacy has already antagonized China, which may no longer have much interest in piped Russian gas, and it has caused a scramble by other actors ranging from China to Turkey and the EU to build rival pipelines that bypass Russia. If the combination of LNG and exploration for shale gas resources in other places, including Poland, Ukraine, and China, should lead to the emergence of a global market for gas, then Russia will be faced with a whole new ball game, one where it will no longer be the unquestioned lead player.

The EU and other outside observers have long been harping on the need for diversification of the Russian economy. There is presently very little in the Russian economy that is worth sinking serious money and effort into, outside the energy complex. But this does not mean that Russia should rest content with pumping and piping.

The way forward should proceed via a wager on high-tech development inside the energy sector. Russian operators should invest heavily in acquiring advanced drilling technology that may unlock offshore riches in the Arctic. They should invest in mastering LNG and thus be in position for the arrival of a global market for gas. They should be thinking seriously about unconventional gas. But none of this is high on the agenda.

Nor do we see any serious efforts to promote efficiency and conservation in domestic energy use, which could make room for expanded exports even at constant levels of production. A case in point is hybrid technology and fuel-efficient cars. China is investing heavily in high-tech battery development for electrical cars; Russia is not. Also, huge amounts of gas are being flared by Russian operators every year simply due to poor coordination between oil and gas producers. According to a report from the World Bank, the amount flared in 2008 was 40 bcm, causing losses to the state of $13 billion and exceeding the total volume of gas flared by Nigeria, Iran, Saudi Arabia, Algeria, and Indonesia combined.[70]

In conclusion, Russian energy policy would seem to leave quite some room for improvement. Retaining our understanding of energy as critical to the future development of Russia, let us look at how a "Russian curse" is hanging over the prospects for serious reform to be undertaken under Putin 2.0.

THE FUTURE OF ECONOMIC REFORM

The main question for the future concerns not only what **needs** to be done, but also and more importantly what can be realistically expected to **be** done. The answer to the former part of the question has been so often repeated that it has taken on an air of mere cliché. The core of the problem is that fixed capital investment is way too low, and the reason given, as indicated previously, is that the investment climate is simply abysmal. Unless there is a change for the better, investors will not commit their money, and enterprises will stand little to no chance of succeeding in the global marketplace. Russia will then be reduced to the ignominious role of a raw materials appendix to the more developed economies, notably so to China.

There are eminent grounds for such worry. The times when export of raw materials could serve as a driver for economic growth are long gone. The same can be said for the classic belief that the mere presence of a development gap in relation to the more highly industrialized economies could serve to drive catch-up growth. If Russia is to achieve true integration into the global economy, its rulers need to realize that sustainable economic growth and technological progress must be driven by endogenous factors. A whole set of what Mancur Olson once referred to as "market-augmenting" institutions must be put into place and be secured.[71] These include not only credible enforcement of contracts and property rights, but also incentives for human capital development.

The main reason why both the United States and the EU have good reasons indeed to worry about competition from countries like China and India lies in an ongoing narrowing of the educational gap. European governments in particular have long cherished a belief that European economies may continue thriving in the face of competition from low cost manufacturing countries, simply because of the superiority of their human capital. There is a strong element of denial here. Following decades of heavy human capital investment in India, China, and elsewhere, it is becoming increasingly debatable to what extent European knowledge-intensive production may be kept safe from outside competition. As President Putin moves back into his old digs inside the Kremlin, he needs to ponder this trend. What seems threatening to the Europeans should be simply frightening to Russia.

The magnitude of the challenge that lies before Putin 2.0 may be brought home via a comparison of the respective growth records of Russia and China. Over the nearly 2 decades from 1989 until 2007, the former being the last year of positive economic growth in the

Union of Soviet Socialist Republics, Russia recorded about zero average annual growth. The high rates of growth that made so much media noise during Putin 1.0 actually achieved little more than make up for the hyperdepression during the Yeltsin era. In sharp contrast, China had meanwhile been chalking up close to 10 percent annual growth since 1978.

The most obvious reason behind this stark difference in performance is that investment intensity in the respective cases has been so very different. As we have noted, China invests well over 40 percent of GDP and Russia less than half of that. The core reason why fixed capital investment in Russia remains so low may be explained by the frequent reference to the country's appalling investment climate, which, in turn, is little more than shorthand for the presence of massive corruption. Perhaps the most discouraging lesson from the 4 years of the Medvedev presidency is that, despite much talk about campaigns to root out corruption, this scourge has actually gotten worse, even much worse.

Towards the end of January 2012, the Russian Interior Ministry's economic security department reported that the size of the average bribe in Russia had more than tripled in 2011: "The size of the average bribe and commercial payoff in reported crimes increased more than 250 percent to 236,000 rubles ($7,866)."[72] A couple of weeks later, Interior Minister Rashid Nurgaliyev told a Ministry board meeting that "The average size of a bribe and commercial palm greasing in identified crimes almost quadrupled and reached 236,000 rubles."[73]

At about the same time, the Russian Central Bank reported that net private sector capital outflow for 2011 had reached $84.2 billion. This must have come as something of a shock to the Kremlin, which in July had predicted capital outflow for the year as a whole at $35 billion. Capital flight had peaked at $133.7 billion in 2008, when the global financial crisis erupted, and dropped to $56.1 billion in 2009, when Russia was coming out of the crisis. In 2010, it had been reduced further, to $33.6 billion, and hopes had been that 2011 would stay at about the same level.[74]

The sharp deterioration provided a clear indication of the sensitivity of investors to political uncertainty. Close to half of the total outflow for 2011, or $37.8 billion, left in the fourth quarter, following the announcement that Putin would return to the Kremlin.[75] The outflow continued in the new year, with $35 billion leaving in the first quarter and an additional $8 billion in April.[76] Although the Russian economy is fundamentally very healthy, with positive growth and an insignificant debt burden, markets clearly remain wary of political risk.

Compared to Russia's GDP of close to $1.5 trillion, the numbers, as such, are not very large. It may be argued that capital outflow is positive in the sense of relieving inflationary pressures. But if the Russian current account should turn negative in 2013, as many expect, then something will have to be done in earnest to ensure that capital remains and is invested within the country. The question is what should be done.

The most immediate needs for action are felt in the realm of fiscal policy. Over the short term, a policy of cautious borrowing, careful spending cuts, and increased taxes may serve to postpone an inevitable return to fiscal prudence. But all are fraught with danger. Given Russia's low ratio of debt to GDP, markets will be only too happy to lend even substantial sums. But a return to mounting debt will also bring increased political dependence, which is clearly not to Putin's liking. Spending cuts would also be welcomed by markets but carry the risk of antagonizing important groups that voted for Putin, who may need their support again before too long. Increasing taxes is clearly in the cards, especially given what Putin has said about a pending "tax maneuver."[77] As noted earlier, Gazprom has already been targeted, and more may follow for the energy sector at large. Yet, raised taxes carry the risk of choking off badly needed growth and must hence be approached with caution.

While undoubtedly important, the question of getting Russia's fiscal house in order is only part of the greater picture. If more money is going to be invested in the Russian economy, by Russians as well as by outside investors, and if entrepreneurial young Russians are to remain in their native country, serious measures need to be taken to achieve improved governance. This is where we need to return to Olson's call for "market-augmenting" government and to ask what it would take for serious change to result.

The good news from an institutional perspective is that the recent wave of protests from below has created yet another window of opportunity. Important elements of civil society have openly emerged, emboldened by new means of communication that are entailed in various social media. The old social contract between Putin and the emerging middle class has broken down, and demands for formal changes in the rules of the game are being met. The core question concerns whether this may be viewed as the beginning of successful collective action, demanding public goods that go beyond material self-enrichment. The answer is not a promising one.

As so many have already pointed out, the opposition is fragmented. It lacks a both a common cause and a common leader. The remnants of the liberal movement from the Yeltsin era — people like Boris Nemtsov and Grigory Yavlinsky — no longer have the credibility needed. There is a strong risk that when, and if, truly charismatic leaders emerge, they will be driven by a strongly nationalist message. It is true that demands for change in a liberal direction have emerged and will have to be met by the regime. While this is necessary for true change in the nature of the game to result, it is clearly not also sufficient.

Belkovsky may well be right in his claim that we are at the beginning of a new "perestroika," but we should not forget how the old one ended. The main message of institutional analysis is that changes in the formal rules will be successful only when backed up by a corresponding transformation of informal norms — and of enforcement mechanisms. The latter is crucial. The core of the challenge to prospective Russian reformers remains linked to improving economic governance, which in essence boils down to ensuring that there is credible enforcement of the rules of the game.

An important part of the reason the track record to date has been so poor may go back to the beliefs of the early reformers in the role of deregulation as a panacea that would bring about a rapid transition to a high-growth market economy. By focusing so one-sidedly on **government failure,** on getting the "grabbing hand of government" into the "velvet glove of privatization," the reformers blinded themselves to the fact that inattention to the broader challenges of sweeping institutional transformation would produce serious cases of **market failure**. In the absence of a government that may credibly commit to upholding contracts and property rights, it will make little sense to even talk about "market economy." Self-interest seeking, which is the core of the market mechanism, will then be decidedly short-term, often value detracting rather than value adding, and, on the whole, detrimental rather than supportive of the common good.

The persistent failure of the Russian government to appear as a credible third-party enforcer of contracts and of property rights is deeply rooted in Russian tradition. There is no predetermination here, indicating that this will always have to remain the case. But the prominent role of the country's energy complex has served to activate rather than phase out deeply ingrained patterns of behaviour.

In a high-performance market economy, the overwhelming share of all transactions will crucially depend on impartial enforcement of contracts and property rights. In the Russian economy, transactions within the energy complex, and within the raw materials sector more generally, have assumed a clearly hierarchical nature, where enforcement is informal and basically devoid of transparency. What is known in Russia as "authoritarian market economy" has thus evolved into little demand for accountability in government, or indeed for the rule of law.

A central feature of governance in this "market" economy rests in its inability to actually enforce what it dictates. The true test of economic authoritarianism lies in whether the rulers are able to produce by command from above what liberal market forces produce by horizontal coordination. In this crucial test, the Putin regime has proven to be woefully inadequate, and for good reason.

In a political culture where the bureaucracy has wide latitude to obstruct and evade any and all types of proposals for change that go against its own vested interests, the only serious impetus for change can come from heavy government priority and attention. Since the government is not able to credibly maintain more than one priority at the time, the overwhelming focus on the energy complex by the government has entailed a complete lack of attention to other and arguably more important tasks.

The Putin regime has surely been quite happy with its rapid accumulation of wealth from hydrocarbon exports. It may have derived even greater satisfaction from the sense of power and prestige that has been associated with its status as an emerging "energy superpower." But these achievements have not come without a price.

The main conclusion to be drawn here is that pervasive corruption has assumed the role of a veritable linchpin for the system of power. Despite all the authoritarian rhetoric, Russia is not ruled by a strong man, or even by a strong regime. It is ruled by a conglomerate of rent seekers, whose members place short-term personal enrichment above any form of longer-term interest of the state. In a long-term Russian perspective, this is something essentially new, and it may turn out to be deeply destructive.

The role model for the "vertical of power" that Putin has been so fond of was housed in the Communist Party of the Soviet Union (CPSU). It ensured that commands from the center would be acted upon and prevented corruption from developing into a serious threat against the main priorities of the system. The "party of power" that Putin built is none of this. In contrast to the CPSU, which was feared by all, "United Russia" has been subjected to so much public ridicule that, in the end, it had to be kept out of Putin's presidential election campaign. The very absurdity of the thought of publicly branding the CPSU as a "party of crooks and thieves," and getting away with it, may serve to drive the message home. Fake authoritarianism will, in the end, come up short, as will all substitutes.[78]

The essence of the Kremlin conglomerate is that it may be kept together only for as long as the appointed rent manager succeeds in maintaining the balance among and within the predatory elites. This is where we arrive at what some have referred to as a "Russian curse." The role of the country's energy complex has not been to **introduce** a "resource curse." The problems of Russian authoritarianism, corruption, and poor economic governance were well entrenched long before the arrival of the hydrocarbon bonanza. It would also seem hard to argue that Russia today is poorer than it would have been without its energy riches.

The reason the hydrocarbon wealth may yet be viewed as a nemesis of sorts is that the immense riches that have been up for grabs have not only aggravated the inherent forces of greed but promoted rent-seeking behavior that is often value detracting. In important ways, it has also constrained the regime. Despite the low rate of domestic investment and the high rate of capital outflow, the Russian government cannot close borders or even restrict capital flows. This would cause a rebellion within the elite. Despite the sheer size of energy incomes that are diverted into private pockets, the Russian government is equally unable to enforce the state interest in cracking down on corruption. In these senses, the regime is arguably more fragile today than ever before.

114

The ills are well known, and continued harping on what **should** be done in terms of formal changes in the rules of the game will be of little value. Some of these changes may indeed be introduced, but likely to little avail. A serious economic improvement will require a new agreement between the country's ruling and entrepreneurial elites, and that is presently not in the cards. Although the main demand during the big Moscow rallies was for honest elections, what really galvanized the opposition was anger over the brazen way in which the elites have been feathering their own nests. But meeting the call for a serious crackdown on corruption would entail a head-on confrontation, which could trigger a hostile takeover of power.

Returning to the question of what likely **will** be done, we may, in consequence, not realistically expect that there will be much change at all beyond cosmetic redesign. For as long as the price of oil remains high, or even very high, and for as long as the "shale gale" does not rise in force to sweep aside Gazprom, then the Kremlin conglomerate may be kept alive and well. The price to the Russian economy will be measured in increasing "primitivization" and marginalization from global markets. Even the hitherto so important production and export of armaments will soon peak and be eclipsed by other countries, again notably so by China.

Perhaps this is where we may view at least a ray of hope for change. If key members of the elite begin to worry that their own sources of wealth and revenue are under threat, then demands for change may perhaps emerge from within. It was in this light that some preferred to view the presidential candidacy of Mikhail Prokhorov — as a way of championing the case for better governance without radically altering the configuration of power. China may perhaps serve as a role model here.

The key to the economic successes of China lies in having found a way of combining an expanded role for the market with retaining a pervasive role for the state. Corruption in China is in every bit as deeply rooted in history as it is in Russia, and it is certainly not to be taken lightly. Yet, the Chinese form of cohabitation between party, state, and private entrepreneurship has clearly prevented corruption and predatory instincts from eroding the prospects for economic growth and technological change. While self-enrichment has been allowed, the state has kept the predators in line and made sure that the common good of the country's economic development is kept in focus. Rent seeking on the whole has been successfully combined with value adding rather than value detracting behavior.

The pronounced Russian ideology of neoliberal deregulation and hard core individualism has been the very opposite of the Chinese way. By allowing a free rein for the predators, it has sacrificed the interests of the state and placed the economic future of the country in jeopardy. The highly short-term nature of the games that are played in Russia, and the essential lack of cohesion both within and among different segments of the elites, combine to lock the Russian economy into a downward spiral. The fundamental lack of security that so clearly marks the regime is manifested not only in reckless fiscal spending but also in a fear of embarking on any form of much-needed change that might trigger counter reactions.

Perhaps the more business oriented members of the ruling elite will, indeed, come to a realization that even their own revenue streams may soon come under threat. Perhaps this will cause them to lobby for action to be taken, and perhaps this may result in a working cohabitation of private interest in self-enrichment with the state or collective interest in value-added longer-term sustainability. But it will all depend crucially on Putin's acquiescence, and there is little to indicate that he is contemplating anything but to stay the course and to hope for continued life support from world energy demand.

If it does not happen, then the real crunch will come when and if the price of oil takes another steep nosedive. This time round, the magnitude of the fall would be far greater than in 2008-09. There would be little to no reserves available and consequently no room for bailouts from the Russian state. The result would be a scramble for safe havens, to save whatever personal assets can still be kept out of the hands of creditors. With the elites in serious turmoil, this could be the trigger for yet another "time of trouble," at the other end of which we would find a hard core nationalist revival.

ENDNOTES - CHAPTER 3

1. The epithet was first introduced in a February 2011 talk show on the Russian radio station finam.fm, where Navalnyi engaged in debate with United Russia Duma member Evgeny Federov. The debate is available from *www.youtube.com/watch?v=ccE-zCR1ej4*. (In early March 2012, it had received close to a million views.)

2. Available from *navalny-en.livejournal.com/3401.html*.

3. This is laid down in Articles 111 and 177 of the Constitution of the Russian Federation.

4. Available from *en.rian.ru/russia/20111222/170427189.html*.

5. Only hours after being appointed, Putin signed a decree offering Yeltsin immunity from prosecution, a lifetime pension, a government country home, and bodyguards and medical care for him and his family. The wording was formulated to cover "former presidents of the Russian Federation." The Duma subsequently voted to limit the immunity, reintroducing liability for serious crimes committed in office.

6. Allegations about Putin's corrupt past have resurfaced regularly over the years. In the run-up to the March 2012 presidential election, they again came to the fore. His main accuser, democratic politician Marina Salye, died on March 28, 2012, at the age of 77. Her passing caused the issue to take another spin through the global media. See, e.g., *www.guardian.co.uk/world/2012/mar/28/ marina-salye*.

7. The claim was originally made by Russian political expert Stanislav Belkovsky in an interview with the German newspaper *Die Welt*. For details, see *www.guardian.co.uk/world/2007/dec/21/ russia.topstories3*.

8. Quoted from *thomas.loc.gov/home/histdox/fed_10.html*.

9. Available from *www.reuters.com/article/2011/09/24/us-russia-idUSTRE78N0RH20110924*.

10. The latter comment was made on December 15, 2011, during Putin's 4.5-hour-long annual televised call-in show, available from *en.rian.ru/russia/20111215/170273019.html?id=*.

11. This happened when he made an appearance at a martial arts event in Moscow on November 21, 2011. It was a harbinger of things to come and left him visibly taken aback. It has been a big hit on YouTube, see *www.youtube.com/watch?v=QzOhEFU2yFw*.

12. Available from *www.nytimes.com/2012/01/20/world/europe /20iht-letter20.html*.

13. Available from *www.washingtonpost.com/opinions/a-new-perestroika/2012/01/26/gIQAB4aWYQ_story.html*.

14. Available from *rt.com/news/prime-time/russia-defense-bud-get-corruption/*.

15. *St. Petersburg Times*, April 17, 2009.

16. Available from *www.suomenpankki.fi/bofit_en/seuranta/venajatilastot/Pages/default.aspx*.

17. Numbers are available at the respective websites of the Central Bank, see *www.cbr.ru/eng/hd_base/mrrf/)* and of the Ministry of Finance, *seewww1.minfin.ru/en/reservefund/statistics/amount/index.php?id4=5817*. Central Bank reserves include funds in the Reserve Fund.

18. Pekka Sutela, "Forecasting the Russian Economy for 2010-2012," *Russian Analytical Digest*, No. 88, 2010, p. 1.

19. *Ibid.*, p. 3.

20. Clifford G. Gaddy and Barry W. Ickes, "Russia after the Global Financial Crisis," *Eurasian Geography and Economics*, Vol. 51, No. 3, 2010.

21. Composed of the United States, UK, France, Germany, Italy, Canada, and Japan.

22. *Ibid.*

23. Available from *www.rts.ru/s618*.

24. Available from *www.france24.com/en/20100416-russian-billionaires-double-2010-rich-list*. The full list is available from *www.forbes.com/lists/2010/10/billionaires-2010_The-Worlds-Billionaires_Rank.html*.

25. Available from *www.eia.doe.gov/dnav/pet/hist/LeafHandler.ashx?n=PET&s=WEPCURALS&f=W*.

26. Available from *www.cbr.ru/eng/statistics/?Prtid=svs*.

27. *Moscow Times*, April 23, 2009.

28. *Moscow Times*, July 28, 2009.

29. *Moscow Times*, July 27, 2009.

30. Available from *www.suomenpankki.fi/bofit_en/seuranta/vena jatilastot/Pages/default.aspx.*

31. Available from *www.cbr.ru/eng/hd_base/mrrf/?C_mes=01& C_year=2009&To_mes=02&To_year=2012&mode=&x=31&y=5.*

32. Available from *www1.minfin.ru/en/reservefund/statistics/ amount/index.php?id4=5817.*

33. *Moscow Times*, August 2, 2011.

34. Available from *www.imf.org/external/pubs/ft/weo/2010/ update/02/index.htm.*

35. Dmitri Trenin, "Cost of the Matter," *Kommersant*, May 14, 2010.

36. *Moscow Times*, September 12, 2001.

37. Julian M. Cooper, "Of BRICS and Brains: Comparing Russia with China, India, and Other Populous Emerging Economies," *Eurasian Geography and Economics*, Vol. 47, No. 3, 2006.

38. Available from *eng.kremlin.ru/speeches/2009/09/10/1534_ type104017_221527.shtml.*

39. Available from *dimitri-medvedev.com/.*

40. Available from *data.worldbank.org/indicator/NE.GDI. FTOT.ZS.*

41. Clifford G. Gaddy, "The Russian Economy in the Year 2006," *Post-Soviet Affairs*, Vol. 23, No. 1, p. 45, 2006.

42. Clifford G. Gaddy and Barry W. Ickes, "Russia's Virtual Economy," *Foreign Affairs*, September/October 1998.

43. At the end of 2010, the accumulated stock of direct investment into Russia emanating from Cyprus had reached an outstanding $179.2 billion. Next in line was Bermuda at $52.6 billion, and British Virgin Islands at $51.0 billion. Then followed the Netherlands at $40.2 billion, Bahamas at $24.6 billion, and Germany at $23.1 billion. The pattern of returning Russian capital, as opposed to FDI by major industrialized economies, is rather striking. See *www.cbr.ru/eng/statistics/print.aspx?file=credit_statistics/dir-inv_in_country_e.htm&pid=svs&sid=ITM_14544*.

44. Shinichiro Tabata, "The Influence of High Oil Prices on the Russian Economy: A Comparison with Saudi Arabia," *Eurasian Geography and Economics*, Vol. 50, No. 1, 2009, p. 90, fn. 29.

45. Available from *hermitagefund.com/newsandmedia/index.php?ELEMENT_ID=65*.

46. *Moscow Times*, January 25, 2012.

47. Available from *www.nytimes.com/2011/07/27/world/europe/27russia.html*.

48. Available from *blogs.ft.com/beyond-brics/2012/01/27/russia-davos-and-the-rule-of-law/#axzz1p4k4H4oQ*.

49. Available from *www.csmonitor.com/World/Europe/2010/1229/After-Khodorkovsky-verdict-Russia-s-Medvedev-bemoans-business-climate*.

50. Available from *www.rferl.org/content/emigration_blues_russias_sixth_brain_drain/2294463.html*.

51. *St. Petersburg Times*, October 22, 2010.

52. Compared to the same period in the previous year, the third and fourth quarters of 1999 came in at, respectively, 11.4 and 12.0 percent, available from *www.cbr.ru/eng/archive/*.

53. Available from *large.stanford.edu/publications/coal/references/oilprice/urals/*.

54. Available from *www.bp.com/liveassets/bp_internet/globalbp/ globalbp_uk_english/reports_and_publications/statistical_energy_re- view_2011/STAGING/local_assets/pdf/oil_section_2011.pdf.*

55. Fiona Hill, "Russia: The 21st Century's Energy Superpow- er?" *The Brookings Review*, Vol. 20 No. 2, 2002, pp. 28-31.

56. Available from *news.bbc.co.uk/2/hi/8090104.stm.*

57. Edward Lucas, *The New Cold War: How the Kremlin Menaces both Russia and the West*, London, UK: Bloomsbury, 2008.

58. Available from *www.cbr.ru/eng/statistics/print.aspx?file= credit_statistics/crude_oil_e.htm&pid=svs&sid=vt1.*

59. Available from *www.bp.com/liveassets/bp_internet/globalbp/ globalbp_uk_english/reports_and_publications/statistical_energy_re- view_2011/STAGING/local_assets/pdf/oil_section_2011.pdf.*

60. *BP Statistical Review of World Energy*, June 2010, p. 6, avail- able from *www.bp.com/liveassets/bp_internet/globalbp/globalbp_uk_ english/reports_and_publications/statistical_energy_review_2008/ STAGING/local_assets/2010_downloads/statistical_review_of_world_ energy_full_report_2010.pdf.*

61. *Ibid.*, pp. 22, 24.

62. Available from *www.gazprom.com/about/production/ extraction/.*

63. Available from *www.gazprom.com/about/today/.*

64. Available from *www.lngworldnews.com/gazprom-added-re- cord-gas-reserves-in-2011-russia/.*

65. Available from *www.osw.waw.pl/en/publikacje/osw-commen- tary/2012-02-23/gazprom-s-position-russian-gas-market-weakening.*

66. Available from *www.iea.org/weo/docs/weo2011/WEO2011_ GoldenAgeofGasReport.pdf.*

67. *BP Energy Outlook 2030*, London, January 2012, available from *www.bp.com/liveassets/bp_internet/globalbp/STAGING/global_assets/downloads/O/2012_2030_energy_outlook_booklet.pdf.*

68. *BP Statistical Review*, pp. 22, 24.

69. *BP Statistical Review of World Energy*, June 2011, p. 22, available from *www.bp.com/assets/bp_internet/globalbp/globalbp_uk_english/reports_and_publications/statistical_energy_review_2011/STAGING/local_assets/pdf/statistical_review_of_world_energy_full_report_2011.pdf.*

70. Available from *www.jamestown.org/single/?no_cache=1&tx_ttnews%5Btt_news%5D=35735.*

71. Mancur Olson, *Power and Prosperity: Outgrowing Communist and Capitalist Dictatorships*, New York: Basic Books, 2000.

72. Available from *en.rian.ru/crime/20120127/170981823.html.*

73. Available from *www.cdi.org/russia/johnson/russia-average-bribe-up-390.cfm.*

74. Available from *en.rian.ru/business/20120113/170734989.html.*

75. Available from *www.cbr.ru/eng/statistics/print.aspx?file=credit_statistics/capital_e.htm&pid=svs&sid=cvvk.*

76. Available from *www.rferl.org/content/russia_capital_outflow/24580379.html.*

77. Available from *en.rian.ru/business/20120209/171232785.html.*

78. Stephen Holmes, "Never Show Weakness: How Faking Autocracy Legitimates Putin's Hold on Power," Per-Arne Bodin, Stefan Hedlund, and Elena Namli, eds., *Power and Legitimacy – Challenges from Russia*, London, UK: Routledge, 2012.

CHAPTER 4

AUTHORITARIANISM AND MODERNIZATION IN RUSSIA: IS RUSSIA KA-PUTIN?

Harley Balzer

Russia's leaders have repeatedly proclaimed the importance of modernizing the nation's economy and stimulating innovation. Yet, despite a dozen years of laudable rhetoric and, more recently, significant increases in spending for education and science, Russia's economy still overwhelmingly depends on commodity exports. While other BRIC (Brazil, Russia, India, and China) countries have introduced global brands reflecting their growing participation in the global knowledge economy, Russia's global brands are in the natural resources sector. The Soviet Union's highly uneven achievements in education, science, and technology are being dissipated, and it will be exceptionally difficult to reverse the decline. Intensifying global competition in education and science means that Russia's academic community will have to exert a tremendous effort merely to avoid falling further behind. Invoking the reminder that "We launched Sputnik" rings quite hollow after more than 6 decades.

Inside Russia, blame for the decline in education and science is placed squarely on the chaos of the 1990s, inadequate funding from the government, and the difficulty of reforming the Soviet system. The achievements of the Yeltsin era—a modest shift to competitive grant funding, programs to integrate higher education and research, and far greater freedom to travel and interact with foreign colleagues—are dismissed as insignificant.

125

The argument here is that the problems are due far more to political failures and corruption that reinforce the intransigence and self-interest of Russia's epistemic communities than to the Soviet legacy or the difficulties of the transition. Comparison with China and with the former communist countries of Central Europe undermines the Soviet legacy argument: Having begun with a nearly identical system—in the 1950s, the Chinese copied the Soviet Union's education and science institutions quite closely. Yet in just 3 decades, the Chinese have overtaken Germany and Japan to rank second to the United States in publishing articles in international peer-reviewed scientific journals. Russian scientists in 2010 published about the same number of articles in international journals as they did in 1990. China's experience also demonstrates the important effects of openness and internationalization. Chinese who have spent considerable time abroad and then return to China have begun to exert a positive influence on the nation's scientific community, demanding international standards and competition in hiring, promotion, and publishing. In Russia, resistance to internationalization remains fierce.

The organizer of the conference asked us to address three questions: What must be done? What are the obstacles? What will be done, and with what consequences?

The overwhelming priority among a plethora of things that must be done is to diversify the economy. After 12 years of the Vladimir Putin-Dmitry Medvedev tandem, Russia's economy depends more on hydrocarbons that it did in 1999. Russia now needs a price of somewhere between $110 and $130 per barrel of oil to balance its budget.[1] If the price of oil were to drop to $80 per barrel, the Reserve Fund would last

1 year. Diversifying the economy requires changes to the political system (incentives and term limits), reforming educational institutions and research organizations to promote more competition and greater internationalization, and changing the incentive structure for epistemic communities in ways that promote greater competition and internationalization.

The most serious obstacles are corruption and self-interest in the political system, educational and research institutions, and Russia's epistemic communities. Change is almost always demonic, and professionals who achieved secure careers before 1991 have little desire to alter the basic elements of their model. Many of those who wished to live under a different system have left the country. The Chinese experience, and that of most Central European countries, demonstrates that reorienting a Soviet-style system is challenging but not impossible. Russia demonstrates that unless political leaders alter the incentive structures, epistemic communities will continue to do what they are used to doing.

The record of the past 12 years suggests that not much will be done to impose significant reforms on the system but that an enormous amount of money will be spent in the name of reform. Much of this money will be stolen or wasted. Creative people will continue to leave Russia to work elsewhere. Russia will continue to decline as a center of education and research and development (R&D). There will be some notable exceptions, but, overall, the picture is bleak.

This chapter discusses of some of the important differences between the authoritarian regimes in China and Russia. It then turns to the knowledge economy prospects of both countries, focusing on higher education, scientific research, and innovation. The conclusion contrasts Chinese accomplishments in education and science with the continuing decline in Russia. Even if Putin's return as President produces meaningful change in the Russian performance, intense global competition means that modest improvements will not alter Russia's relative position. The changes that are most needed — competition, internationalization, and integration — will require both political change and reorientation of Russia's epistemic communities.

AUTHORITARIANISMS

While Russia and China both remain authoritarian regimes, the character of the authoritarianism differs significantly. Russia's system is highly personalized, with Putin now occupying the sort of position Deng Xiaoping achieved in China in the 1980s and early 1990s. While Deng never codified his status with a corresponding title, Putin has been dubbed Russia's "national leader." Neither system is transparent, but the Chinese system obscures how decisions are reached among a collective leadership,[2] while Russia's system obscures how the top leader determines policy.[3]

The political science community has generated a large body of work on authoritarianism and recently on "upgrading" authoritarianism. The two major conclusions from comparative studies of authoritarian regimes are that 1) single-party regimes perform better and last longer when well institutionalized; and 2) a unified opposition is more likely to defeat incumbents in an electoral democracy.[4] Neither finding is a surprise. But these findings do help explain why incumbents devote significant resources to co-opting a "loyal opposition" and fostering conflict among opponents.[5]

The literature on "authoritarian upgrading" examines in detail the various ways nondemocratic regimes have sought to perpetuate their rule. Much of this literature has been generated by scholars focusing on the Middle East and North Africa,[6] but scholars of China have made significant contributions,[7] as have analysts examining other regions.[8] The menu of policies adopted by these regimes includes:

- containing or crowding out civil society,[9]
- managing political contestation,
- **selective** economic reforms,
- controlling new media and communication technology
- diversifying international linkages, in particular relying on China as both a model and patron, that provide an alternative to Europe, America, or international financial institutions that impose various forms of conditionality.

A paired comparison[10] of Russia and China allows us to examine differences in authoritarian regimes more closely. The comparison is particularly valuable because 1) China modeled so much of its original political and economic system on Soviet institutions; and 2) China is now performing better in the political realm, in economic development, and in education, R&D, and innovation. China's epistemic communities are integrating with their international peers to a far greater extent than those in Russia.[11]

Relative economic performance can be seen in a comparison of economic output growth in the past 5 years (see Table 4-1):

	Russia	China
2008	5.6	9.6
2009	-9.0	8.7
2010	3.6	10.0
2011	3.4	9.7
2012 (projected)	3.5	7.5

Table 4-1. Economic Output Growth.

China has conducted a major evaluation of the causes of Soviet implosion and examined authoritarian regimes elsewhere.[12] This stunning example of a regime learning how to improve its authoritarian institutions has resulted in significant changes, including:

- A form of "market-preserving federalism that has allowed enormous leeway for (at least some) regions to find their own paths to successful economic development.[13]
- Term and age limits constraining how long political leaders may serve.
- Expansion and improvements in education, with a major emphasis on internationalization.[14] When the new Central Committee is announced in 2012, some 20 percent of the members will have foreign higher education credentials (overwhelmingly advanced degrees, though this will change over time to increase the proportion with foreign bachelor of arts degrees.)[15]
- Merit plays growing role in cadre selection. It is not the sole criterion, and family and *guanxi* relationships continue to be extremely important. But the Chinese appear to have established a

"floor" of basic competence for officials, with intense competition forcing them to produce results.[16]

- Party discipline continues to play a role, providing a way to keep corruption within a poorly defined but nevertheless enforced set of limits.[17]

- Finally, the leadership is not only aware of the major challenges facing the regime (regional and sectoral economic imbalances, demography, information society, and corruption), but has been adopting specific measures to confront these difficulties. The process has been slow and uneven, with tremendous resistance from those reaping benefits from the existing system. Much will depend on the willingness of the new leadership to push for needed changes.[18]

In contrast, Russia's leaders have done little to institutionalize the post-Boris Yeltsin system. Rather, Putin (like his Soviet and Tsarist forebears) seems to have determined that institutional strictures impose limits on his political power. While abiding by the letter of Russia's laws, he rejects their spirit. The system is reminiscent of Fyodor Dostoyevskii's Grand Inquisitor dream sequence, which suggested that people would always exchange freedom for bread, miracle, mystery, and authority. It is codified in Vladislav Surkov's (Putin's so-called grey cardinal and the architect of much of the regime's ideology and domestic policy in 2000-08) writings about "sovereign democracy." Those writings state that Russia must never be in a position where other countries could dictate what sort of political, social, or economic system the country would have.[19] Hence, any time sovereignty is limited, the country could not possibly be a democracy. One of many major problems with the concept of sovereign democracy is that it was developed with no public input. It reflects one individual's assessment of what the country needs or wants.

Putin's system may be described as increasingly managed pluralism.[20] In various realms, the government endeavors to keep up (technology and the Internet); crowd out (civil society); and blame "others" ("democrats," Yeltsin, the West). This approach came close to failing during the 2011-12 election cycle and is now undergoing some revision, mostly in the direction of legislative changes that limit freedoms, changes in electoral laws that are designed to maintain the advantages enjoyed by the "party of power," new and repressive police measures and laws against dissidents, and new controls over the media, including new media.

One way in which the relative success of Chinese "upgrading" may be measured is by comparing the perceived legitimacy of the two regimes. Both societies experience significant amounts of protest. But in China, blame is focused overwhelmingly on local officials, **NOT on the Chinese Communist Party (CCP) or the regime**. The Chinese version of authoritarian upgrading has managed some degree of both capitalism and accountability without democracy. In contrast, Russia's "power vertical" creates a situation where it is nearly impossible to shift blame to others: Moscow makes all the significant decisions and controls the distribution of rents. It is difficult to blame others when the "national leader" is a self-proclaimed control freak. The system produces rigidity but not accountability.

Russia was the worst-performing member of the G20 during the economic crisis after 2008. By 2011, the problems were clear, and more serious difficulties were avoided only by a modest (and perhaps temporary) recovery in oil prices. Meanwhile, other associated symptoms of decay are visibly manifesting themselves:

- Food prices are rising.
- Agriculture is suffering.
- The natural resource model of economic development is viewed as defunct.
- The Putin-Medvedev "tandem" is considered to have been just a show.
- There are tangible signs of real elite concern.[21]

However, it is not clear that differences among Russia's elites are genuine:

- A popular joke in Moscow during Medvedev's Presidency was that each leader had a strong team of advisors, that these advisors had both personal and substantive differences of opinion, and that the differences could translate into quite different policies. The one thing that was not clear was to which team Medvedev belonged.
- The alleged difference of opinion between Putin and Medvedev over Libyan policy could have been staged, allowing Russia to keep lines open to both sides.
- The tandem appears to have been designed to appeal to different audiences both inside and outside Russia: Medvedev to the educated and the new middle class; Putin to nationalists and blue collar workers. Medvedev developed a good relationship with Obama; Putin focused on the near abroad and China.
- The difficulties and protests provoked some splits in the elite, but serious questions remain

regarding how independent "opposition" figures like Alexei Kudrin and Mikhail Prokhorov really are.

It is evident that at least some portions of the elite view Putin's economic model as having reached a dead end. The broader public has been less motivated or mobilized, but even before the election campaign began, the regime was subjected to increasing criticism and satirized with growing sharpness. Corruption, in particular, has been a target. Opposition blogger Aleksei Navalnyi's characterization of United Russia as the "Party of Thieves and Scoundrels" acquired a life of its own. Groups within the elite generated a number of reports critical of the political and economic system.

For example, Medvedev's own think tank, INSOR, issued a report that, not surprisingly, called for Medvedev to remain in the presidency. The Center for Strategic Development produced a document covering many of the same concerns and ended by invoking the need for a "third man" to assume the nation's leadership. Vladimir Milov, Boris Nemtsov, and Mikhail Kasyanov published a report called "Putin. Corruption," demanding change at the top. What is striking about all of these critiques is that they focus on personalities rather than institutions.[22]

Lilia Shevtsova is correct that only pressure from below will force real change.[23] But pressure from below alone is more likely to produce violent/revolutionary change. A peaceful transition to democracy requires a balance of supply and demand: pressure from below must demand democracy, and some effective portion of the elite must be willing to supply it. This is why **consolidated,** as opposed to electoral or illiberal democracy, remains the exception among political regimes. Michael McFaul got it badly wrong when he wrote about democrats creating democracies and authoritarians establishing authoritarian regimes.[24] The key is devising institutional structures that force even "sham" democrats to continue to behave according to democratic rules. This requires both an institutional structure that precludes absolute power and an opposition willing to enforce the rules.

The Russian protests in late 2011 and early 2012 were a surprise to just about everyone. But there **were** warnings that the population had become less complacent. Most observers missed or dismissed these warnings. This was easy to do when Putin's regime consistently emphasized the absence of alternatives, and the protests that occurred remained focused on specific issues rather than more general political demands. This changed on September 24, 2011, when Putin let it be known that he was returning to the Presidency. Even if he could claim that he would win an election against any possible opponent (and, of course, serious opponents were barred from becoming candidates), the manner in which this was done made it clear that a "selectorate" of one had taken the decision. To many Russians, this was an insult. Putin's behavior was ill-advised, given the changes in Russia's political landscape over the previous 8 years.

Studies of the 2003-04 election cycle generally have emphasized the greater margin of victory for both United Russia and Putin.[25] United Russia did, indeed, increase its majority in the Duma in 2003, and in March 2004, Putin won by a far more comfortable margin than in 2000. But turnout declined when compared to the 1999-2000 electoral cycle, and the vote "against all" was notably greater in both December 2003 and March 2004.[26] This induced the regime to change the electoral rules, abolishing minimum turnout requirements and removing the "against all" option from ballots.

Monetization of social benefits produced protests in 80 of Russia's then 89 regions during January to March 2005. Russian motorists staged protests in Vladivostok over limits on auto imports. After a speeding car carrying the governor of Altai rammed another vehicle and killed the governor, the driver of the car that was struck was put on trial, provoking protests in Altai and many other regions. Similar incidents elsewhere of cars using official blue lights to evade traffic jams and causing accidents generated the *"migalki"* (blue bucket) protests, with people wearing buckets on their heads.

In late-2010, protests in Samara, Irkutsk, and Kaliningrad demanded removal of governors and local governments. The protest in Kaliningrad by "Spravedlivost'" on January 30, 2010, was the largest public demonstration in Russia since 1991. In Moscow, Strategy 31 activists staged protests on the 31st day of each month with a "31st" to protest violations of Article 31 of the Russian Constitution guaranteeing freedom of assembly.[27]

One of the most direct warnings about popular dissatisfaction came in two reports from Mikhail Dmitriev's Center for Strategic Research, the first in March and the second in November 2011.[28] Based on focus groups, Dmitriev and his colleagues found significant resentment of both personalities and policies. Dmitirev's claims for the superiority of focus groups over survey research are rejected by many behavioral sociologists, and his team did not recruit focus groups outside major cities. Nevertheless, he did sound an important warning.

Survey data from the Levada Center also should have provided a warning regarding any effort to manipulate the legislative elections. Its poll in August of 2011 found that 64 percent of Russians wanted to see "significant" or "complete" turnover in the Duma. (See Figure 4-1.)

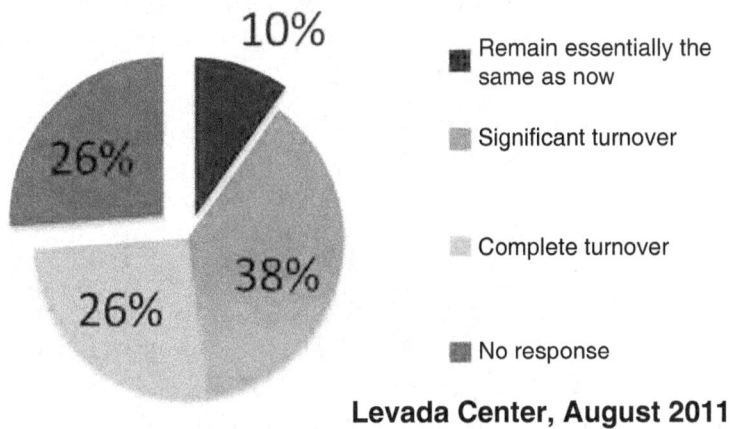

Levada Center, August 2011

Figure 4-1. Percentages of Desired Turnover in Russian DUMA.

Given the spread of dissatisfaction, it is legitimate to ask why and how the regime has managed to remain intact through the economic crisis that began in 2008. Analysts have pointed to Putin's popularity, oil rents, and the overwhelming weight of regions and population groups that depend on the government's redistribution policies. Natalia Zubarevich's discussion of multiple Russias has become extremely popular.[29] My concern with this analysis is that it treats regions and population groups as monolithic, rather than exploring their diversity. Even in the company towns that depend most on the government, some individuals have expressed alternative opinions. Mayoral elections in four cities in early 2012 produced outcomes that rejected the United Russia incumbents.[30] Even if many smaller towns are overwhelmingly pro-Putin and inclined to seek support from Moscow rather than challenge the government, not everyone adheres to this view. The Levada Center data showing that nearly two-thirds of Russians wanted to see "significant" or "complete" turnover in the Duma should give us pause in assuming that the overwhelming majority of Russians accept the status quo.

A second prevalent myth is that protest is entirely rooted in economic conditions.[31] This makes oil prices the key to regime survival. This view, rooted in Soviet-era materialism, ignores the impact of at least four other factors: dignity, fatigue, ideology, and specific policies.

The Arab Spring began in Tunisia not because of bread riots or price shocks, but because Mohammed Bouazizi immolated himself after being humiliated by a female police officer. People who feel that their basic dignity has been assaulted may, at times, behave in ways that political scientists or sociologists would consider irrational. Dignity is one of the crucial common elements in both the Arab Spring and the protests over Russia's elections.

Fatigue with long-serving leaders is another important trigger. Hosni Mubarak lasted 3 decades before Egyptians decided that they had had enough. Putin was less fortunate: a significant share of the Russian population did not welcome his return to the Kremlin. Ideology got a bad name from the Union of Soviet Socialist Republic's (USSR) use and abuse of Marxism, and liberalism suffered from the economic decline in the 1990s. Nevertheless, human rights remain a powerful mobilizing force. Some Russians have learned enough about the world to demand legality, an end to corruption, and, in some cases, even democracy.

Russians across the country have shown a willingness to protest against specific policies. If leaders

emerge who are able to connect these specific grievances to more general issues of the political system,
the chemistry could be combustive. *Khimki, migalki,
l'goty,* and other protests could ignite a wider fire. If
the case is made that each of these represents not an
isolated instance, but rather is the product of a system
that does not permit adequate societal input regarding important policy decisions, the system itself could
be called into question.

Epistemic Communities.

In addition to lack of leadership, an important reason why the local protests have not (yet?) generated
effective demands for change in the political system
involves the role of Russia's epistemic communities.
While criticism and attention have focused on political
and economic policies and top-level leaders, many of
the most intractable problems in Russia involve professional groups and individual professionals that, for
reasons of self-interest and investment in Soviet practices, continue to reject genuine internationalization.
This can be seen in demography, education, science
and medicine, and innovation/R&D.[32]

Professional demographers have long warned
that Russia faces a serious population decline. Yet
Putin's regime continues to rely on the projections of
critics of "Western" demography, who assert that the
government's combination of propaganda and "maternity capital" payments has successfully reversed
Russia's population decline.[33] A more sober analysis
of the situation notes that the increase in births over
the past 5 years is due to an increase in the number of
women aged 20-29, the cohort most likely to have children. The maternity capital program appears to have

encouraged women to have children sooner, to make sure they can take advantage of the program before economic conditions change, but has not had a significant impact on the total fertility rate (TFR), the indicator that is key to reversing population decline. In one of his election campaign articles, Putin stated that his regime would raise the TFR to 1.73 by 2015. It is not clear just how this will be accomplished, and offering a number to three decimal places raises eyebrows.

The majority of Russian professionals, or at least their leadership, continue to adhere to belief systems and incentive systems inherited from the Soviet era. The result is a growing divorce from international professional communities. It is not total separation. Many Russian specialists keep up with global developments and collaborate with foreign colleagues. But a significant share of the professionals prefer the comfort and apparent security of doing things the way they have done them for decades. This is particularly the case for leaders of "legacy" organizations carried over from the Soviet era.

The consequences of Russia's "thin" internationalization are apparent in education, science and technology, and innovation/R&D. The situation is thrown into particularly stark relief if Russia's performance since 1991 is compared to China's since 1978. In the 1950s, China adopted the Soviet systems of education, science, and technology almost completely, and received significant assistance from the USSR in doing so.[34] If China, starting from a much lower base, has succeeded in reorienting the components of its knowledge economy to become a major player in global science and education, while Russia continues to dissipate the Soviet legacy in education and science, this suggests that policy, rather than the systemic legacy or path dependency, is the key factor. The epistemic communities in both countries continue to play an important role in the policies that have been adopted.

Starting points of reform, rather than history, mentality, or institutions, may be the key factor explaining the difference. China began "reform and openness" following the disastrous decade of the Cultural Revolution. Epistemic communities were fragmented, with many individuals "sent down" to the countryside. Professional groups in China were not in a position to assert claims to expertise when Deng initiated reform. In contrast, Mikhail Gorbachev introduced perestroika when the USSR could claim to be a co-equal superpower. Soviet/Russian professionals believed that their practices, knowledge base, and skills were as good as (or better than) any in the world. Where Chinese specialists sought to learn as much as possible from the developed countries, with the goal of eventually learning enough to become leaders, many Russian professionals felt that there was little the foreigners could teach them. Many who did value foreign models have left the country, a trend Putin continues to encourage. While the Chinese embraced globalization as a way to catch up and overtake the developed countries, many Russians view globalization as an American project designed to inhibit their development. The result is that China has internationalized in stunning ways, while Russia has resisted international integration in equally stunning ways.[35]

Education.

In creating a modern knowledge economy, Russia is stymied by myths about its Soviet past. All the rhetoric about the "scientific-technical revolution" obscured serious problems in education, science and technology, and innovation. In education, Soviet achievements in a few fields produced complacency rather than a sense that the world is highly competitive and requires constant effort just to avoid falling further behind. Since the demise of the USSR, Russia has become a world leader in the proportion of the population enrolled in higher education. Unfortunately, the quality of that education remains uneven, and the standards for awarding degrees have been seriously compromised.[36]

Both Russia and China have significantly increased the number of students receiving higher education. Growth in China has been tremendous, though starting from a much lower base. Russia now has a larger share of its population receiving higher education than any other country in the world. Annual admissions to higher education exceed the number of high school graduates.[37] However, about half of the students are enrolled in correspondence divisions of higher education institutions, and another 10 percent are in evening divisions. Less than half study full time. (See Table 4-2.)

Russia		China	
1990	2,824,500 (2 percent)	1997	1,000,000
2008	7,513,000 (5 percent)	2006	5,500,000

Table 4-2. Higher Education Enrollments.

Russia has probably reached the peak of higher education enrollments, given that the number of high school graduates will decline each year until 2017. China announced a target of 30,000,000 students to be enrolled in higher education by 2010, though this figure undoubtedly includes secondary specialized as well as higher education institutions.

Rapid expansion in any education system raises questions of quality, and this is a serious concern in both countries. One significant issue is that in both systems, the number of faculty has not kept pace with the increases in enrollments. As Table 4-3 shows, the number of faculty has grown by 66 percent, while student enrollments have increased by 165 percent. (The faculty data includes *sovmetitelstvo*, the practice of individuals teaching at more than one institution. This was a common practice in Tsarist Russia, due to low salaries. Stalin banned it. It returned after 1991, again due to low salaries.)

In both the Chinese and Russian systems, the response to concerns about quality and poor performance in an environment of finite resources has been to focus on a limited number of "elite" institutions. China's 211 program has identified 106 higher education institutions, with nine of them receiving top priority. In Russia, the government has chosen 29 research universities through competitions and selected an additional 10 federal universities. The Research University project began with two pilot institutions, and the government then conducted two open competitions, selecting 27 more universities. The Federal University program also began with two pilot projects, one in Krasnoyarsk and one in the Southern Federal District. The Russian government subsequently named an additional six institutions. Moscow State University and St. Petersburg State University have maintained their special status, bringing the number of federal universities to 10.[38]

The difference in the selection process for the two types of institutions reflects an effort to balance competing priorities. In selecting the research universities, quality was supposed to be the main consideration. However, the author's personal experience participating in several rounds of competitions for special status and funding for universities indicates that it is nearly impossible to eliminate the issue of regional distribution from consideration.[39] The federal universities were selected on the basis of regional needs. The absence of any competition, or even a requirement that the institutions provide a plan for what they would do differently with their new status, raises concerns that reform is not on the agenda. Even if some administrators have thoughts about significant change, the process of amalgamating several previously independent institutions with their own physical plant, faculty, administration, and traditions will occupy their attention for several years.

A great deal of money is being spent, but much of it for construction, equipment, and other infrastructure. In Russia, this process rarely involves competitive bidding, and opportunities for corruption and waste are widespread. Inefficiency in using the new funding also derives from rigid bureaucratic controls over how money is allocated and what it may be used for. Often, funds are provided late in the fiscal year but must be spent before the year's end. In one case, a rector of a university sent practically every member of the university faculty on a business trip (*komandirovka*) to use funds that arrived late in the calendar year. This probably did more to help Aeroflot and Russian Railways than to improve higher education.

Among the most striking differences between Russian and Chinese higher education is the character of internationalization. The Chinese have embraced educational globalization; Russia's academic community remains more wary. Russian concerns were clearly visible in discussions about the Bologna Process (a series of ministerial meetings and agreements between European countries designed to ensure comparability in the standards and quality of higher education qualifications) in the late 1990s and early 2000s. The rector of Moscow University, Viktor Antonovich Sadovnichy, initially stated that Russia had the best universities in the world and therefore should eschew involvement in Bologna. Liudmila Alekseevna Verbitskaia, rector of St. Petersburg University, shared the evaluation of Russia's world leadership, but her interpretation of its meaning was that Russia should participate in the Bologna process in order to have maximum influence over the project. Press accounts in the 2000s and several dozen personal interviews with university administrators suggest that Sadovnichy's opinion is widely shared, though he has altered his view over time.

Results of the Chinese embracing internationalization, while the Russians remain hesitant, may be seen in international rankings, treatment of faculty with foreign degrees, and the role of returnees. Russian higher education has nearly vanished from international rankings. In 2009, *The Times of London* included five institutions from Hong Kong (ranked 24, 35, 46, 124, and 195) and six from mainland China (ranked 49, 52, 103, 153, 154, and 168) in its ranking of the world's top 200 higher education institutions. Russia placed only two on the list, Moscow State University (155) and St. Petersburg State University (168). After *The Times* altered its criteria to accord less weight to reputation beginning in 2010, Russian institutions vanished from the top 200. In 2012, Moscow University had dropped into a tie with 25 other institutions at 276; St. Petersburg University was tied with 49 other institutions at 351.[40]

One response has been for Russians to produce their own rankings. A first effort in this direction produced much more satisfactory results for Russian institutions: Moscow and St. Petersburg ranked in the top 100 (Moscow at 5); no Chinese institutions ranked in the top 100; the second 100 included two Russian, two Chinese, and two Hong Kong institutions. The truly stunning data came in the ranking of numbers 300-430. Here, 45 Russian higher education institutions were included among the 130 on the list. Overall, the Russian ranking system included 52 Russian institutions among the world's top 430, or 12 percent. These results reflect the criteria used for the rankings, which included the number of specialties, number of students, and number of alumni. Small, specialized, or liberal arts institutions were clearly not going to rank well in this system.

The Russian government has announced plans to establish an "official" ranking system, using its own criteria. This fits a pattern of Russia reacting to globalization by insisting on different rules, rather than endeavoring to mesh with the global trends. Scholars at the Moscow State Institute for International Relations developed an alternative to the Davos rankings. Russia's Finance Ministry has its own criteria for identifying global financial centers. The Russian Academy of Sciences insists on its own methodology for determining scientific productivity.

The Chinese, too, have begun to publish their own rankings. In contrast to Russia, they downplay their own institutions. While Moscow University ranked in the top 100 higher education institutions in the Chinese Jiao Tong rankings, no Chinese institutions were included. In interviews, Chinese academics have offered contradictory explanations for downplaying the quality of Chinese higher education institutions. Some have stated that it is a budget game, permitting administrators to demand more funds to raise the quality of Chinese institutions. Others say that it is a combination of modesty and a desire to show results over a longer period of time: if in 5-10 years their institutions begin to rise in the Chinese global rankings, this will be evidence of their good performance.[41]

Another measure of internationalization is the number of foreign-trained faculty teaching at universities and institutes. Chinese higher education institutions welcome both Chinese and foreigners with postgraduate degrees from foreign institutions. In Russia, it has been difficult to overcome a legacy of not recognizing foreign degrees. Russian rules prohibited anyone from teaching for more than 3 years unless the person earned a Russian credential (*Kandidat* or *Doktor*

Nauk-DR. of Sciences). These rules have been relaxed for scholars chosen in the two recent competitions for "mega grants" at Russian universities, but resistance to recognizing foreign degrees remains strong. It is one of the intensely debated issues in Russia's participation in the Bologna process.

A large number of students from both China and Russia go abroad. Deng insisted that China had to allow students to go abroad, even if some of them would never return. Despite consistently over-estimating the proportion that would return, he did not waver from the policy. Estimates of the number of Chinese who went abroad for higher education vary, since many paid their own way and were not involved in official Chinese study abroad programs. Beginning around 2005, there was a shift from the dominant group being graduate students to a larger number of undergraduates, reflecting interest in foreign training and the greater capacity of Chinese families to fund the education.[42]

The majority of Chinese students who have studied abroad have not returned. Estimates suggest that perhaps 20-30 percent have opted to work in China. Even that relative small proportion of returnees had exerted a significant impact on the Chinese education and research systems. The process has not been free of problems. China has encountered conflicts between the "sea turtles" who go abroad and the "land turtles" who remain in China.[43] Yet a growing body of evidence suggests that the returnees have exerted a significant positive effect on Chinese institutional development, standards, and internationalization. Koen Jonkers describes a "virtuous circle" in the life sciences,[44] and Dan Brenitz and Michael Murphree note positive contributions in the information technology (IT) sector (even if this has not yet generated new product innovation).[45]

In Russia, the returnees have thus far exerted little impact. A new program to offer mega grants to about 200 leading Russian and international scholars has conducted two rounds of competition and a third round in 2012. Thus far, the program has made fewer than 100 awards. For the first time, Russian higher education institutions (VUZy) are allowing leading specialists to copy the model of China's "swallows," spending 4 months in Russia and the rest of their time in their home countries. How much impact these 200 scholars will be able to have remains an important open question. Once again, a large amount of money is being spent with little guarantee of measurable results.

Foreign student enrollments are another indication of the degree of educational internationalization. Russia enrolls about 100,000 foreign students. About 40 percent come from former Soviet republics (half from Kazakhstan), and another 40 percent from Asia (the majority from China). China enrolls more than three times as many foreign students, with the top sending countries being South Korea, Japan, the United States, Vietnam, and Thailand.

China is not only sending more students abroad, but is also reaping greater benefits from those who return. In 2001, neither Russia nor China ranked as a major donor nation in the number of students studying abroad (defined by the Institute for International Education as those on official programs that implied eventual return to the home country). By 2006, China was ranked 6th in the world in the number of students studying abroad, with 6 percent of the total global flow, behind Australia with 7 percent and Germany with 8 percent but ahead of Canada and Japan (both with 4 percent). Russia continued to be absent from the list of top sending nations. A growing number of Russian young people studying abroad enroll directly in foreign institutions, rather than participating in official exchange programs.

The shift to mass tertiary education in Russia has placed a growing burden on students. About two-thirds of the students enrolled at state institutions now pay tuition.[46] Competition for the "budget" places that offer free tuition and a stipend has become so thoroughly corrupted at some VUZy that parents question whether it might be less expensive for their children to enroll in the "commercial" division and pay the tuition rather than spending even more money on tutors and side payments to gain a "budget" place (personal communications). While educational services have become marketized, there is not yet much price competition among VUZy.[47] This may change in the coming decade, as the number of potential applicants continues to decline. The cost of tuition is increasing, due to inflation and also due to a formula that ties the amount a VUZ may charge for tuition to the amount spent on budget students. As the government has increased the funding for state VUZy, this raises the amount of spending per student and therefore the price for those paying tuition. Greater monetization inevitably generates more corruption and fraudulent behavior. Data indicate that Russian families spend even more on side payments for education than for medical care.[48]

The new economics of higher education in Russia is not sustainable. The demographic situation means that VUZy will increasingly need to compete for students. Weaker institutions will have difficulty as the applicant pool shrinks. The key question is whether all institutions will try to survive with a smaller enrollment, which means less funding from tuition, or whether the number of institutions will contract.[49]

Decline in the education system, despite (or because of) the greater number of students presages continuing difficulties in science and technology (S&T), and in R&D. These challenges, in turn, will make it difficult for Russia to play a role in global systems of production and innovation.

Science and Technology.

One of the most stunning changes of the past 2 decades has been the rapid and unexpected loss of scientific capacity in Russia.[50] The Soviet Union's achievements in science and technology may have been overstated, but there is no question that, in some fields, the USSR made major contributions to world science.[51] This has changed markedly since the 1980s. In part, it reflects the disruptions and lack of funding in the 1990s — the explanations that leaders of Russia's scientific community prefer to emphasize. But it also stems from significant losses of personnel and a failure to reorient the Soviet system to function in the global knowledge economy competition that dominates education and S&T in the 21st century. The two factors are related: an exodus of many of the best younger scholars in the 1990s removed people who were both the rising stars of Russian science and a major force for greater international integration. Those who remained in Russia were those who were less able to compete in the global market for science talent or those who genuinely preferred the Soviet system. Certainly not all the talented scientists emigrated. But enough of the "best and the brightest" did depart to cede control over science to researchers and administrators with less interest in changing the system.

In the global competition in education and S&T, Russia confronts many challenges that are similar to other nations: these include the costs of mass tertiary education, demands of the knowledge economy, and constraints on available resources to fund competing priorities. But Russia is also an outlier in important ways: the demographic crisis; the continuing role of the Academy of Sciences; bureaucratic obstacles; failure to confront fraud and corruption; and, most striking, resisting internationalization. In many of these areas, and particularly in resisting international norms, epistemic communities play a crucial and often detrimental role. The combination of the Soviet knowledge base and self-interest (institutional, career, and financial) induces many Russian scientists and science administrators to resist a Russian version of "reform and openness."

Other former socialist countries have encountered similar dilemmas. In Hungary, Poland, and other Eastern members of the European Union (EU), the Academies of Science continue to play a major and sometimes disruptive role. But each of these countries has managed to move toward a greater role in global innovation processes.[52] In China, the battle has been long and difficult. But in most of the other former communist countries, a combination of government policy, professional self-interest, and international influences have produced a shift to competition and internationalization. In Russia, the process has been halted and, in many places, reversed.

The data on Russian decline is overwhelming. Whether in terms of peer-reviewed scientific publications, number of researchers, number of advanced degrees, patent filings, or the related realms of utility model and industrial design applications, Russia's performance has stagnated or declined since 1990. China's rankings have shot up to the point where China now ranks second to the United States in scientific publications in international peer-reviewed journals.[53] When presented with these data, the president of Russia's Academy of Sciences responded by stating that Russia publishes many good journals and suggested foreign researchers should learn Russian so that they could read this valuable literature (personal communication). In early 2012, Russian science officials announced that they were developing their own version of a science citation index that would include the in-house publications favored by Russian institutes and the summaries of reports given at professional meetings (*tezisy dokladov – Thesis Report*).

Peer review, which increased in prevalence in the 1990s, has become less used and is not a factor in the new index. (In 1993, when the author directed George Soros's International Science Foundation, several rounds of grant competition based on peer review were conducted. At the time, Boris Saltykov, Minister of Science of the Russian Federation, mandated that peer review would be the way to distribute any new funds that became available to his Ministry. The Academy of Science has resisted the switch from administrative allocation to competition, and in the 2000s has been successful at cutting back on peer-reviewed competitions as a way to award research support.)

Innovation.

The weakening Russian capacity in education and research is exacerbating a serious innovation deficit inherited from the Soviet era. Despite incessant invocation of *vnedrenie* (innovation), the Soviet system performed poorly in developing new technology. The widely heralded success in launching Sputnik was, we now know, neither a major technological breakthrough nor a result of a long-term state.[54] Accounts of Soviet technology demonstrate two important lessons. First, the military did perform better, but it accomplished this due to priority rather than overseeing a separate, more advanced R&D complex.[55] Some highly talented individuals did seek the rewards of working for the Soviet military industrial complex; other highly talented individuals consciously sought to avoid the security restrictions and constraints military work involved, knowing that secrecy would cut them off from their international colleagues. Second, the Soviet Union did export technology, but what it exported consisted overwhelmingly of basic instruments. In machine tools, for example, the USSR exported a much larger number of units than it imported, but the value of the imports far exceeded that of the exports. Exports consisted of first and second generation basic metal cutting and grinding equipment; imports were expensive, sophisticated, numerically-controlled tools (e.g., the famous case of the Toshiba machines and submarine propellers that allowed the Soviets to manufacture quiet propellers).

Many now assert that Russia has switched from being one gigantic military industrial complex to being a petrostate. Innovation in resource-producing countries is most successful when it begins in the natural resource sectors.[56] While there is some evidence that this is beginning to happen in a few Russian regions, the government's emphasis has been overwhelmingly on the high-technology realms that Putin mistakenly believes were the Soviet Union's crown jewels.[57] To focus on IT, high technology, and nanotechnology in a country that never achieved serial production of a personal computer is a tall order.

The Soviet Union had three separate systems of R&D: the Academy of Sciences, higher education, and industrial facilities. There was little integration among them. The industrial R&D system has largely vanished, as most enterprises either do not make a profit or earn too little to be able to support R&D activities. In data regarding spending on science, Russia does not rank badly in terms of government support (29th in world in share of gross domestic product [GDP]), but Russian industry lags seriously in what it contributes. In Organization for Economic Cooperation and Development (OECD) countries, about two-thirds of R&D is funded by industry; in Russia, the figure is just 27 percent.[58] One relative bright spot has been a significant increase in support for research at higher educational institutions, but the new equipment and grant programs have not yet produced significant returns.

The Academy of Sciences remains in a serious crisis. In the Soviet Union, science is viewed as "a system for generating knowledge," rather than as a realm with serious real-world applications. The purview of "science policy" did not include technology or innovation.[59]

Personnel have become a significant problem in the Academy and in academia, with a rapidly aging scientific community. Due to emigration, scientists in the

40-59 age group are a far smaller cohort than would normally be expected (one-half the proportion in the United States, while those over 60 are three times the share among American scientists). The extensive and continuing brain drain, both internal and external, remains a serious problem. Stifling bureaucracy and rampant corruption are major reasons for this exodus and have a significant impact on those who remain in Russia. Here again, the processes are mutually reinforcing: the scientists most likely to demand better management, competition, and honesty in attributing work to authors are often the ones most inclined to leave the country.

Russia is hardly the only country to experience a significant brain drain, but it reaps far less of a "brain gain" than most other developing or developed economies and participates less in global "brain circulation." The vast majority of Russian scientists who have left the country are not inclined to return (recent Nobels). Compared to China, the programs to attract talent from abroad, whether returnees or foreigners, are modest and insulated. Russia has generally resisted the "swallow" model of researchers spending a few months each year in the country, something the Chinese regard as unavoidable.

The new competitive grants that have been introduced are small. The funds often are paid late in the fiscal year. Some scientists who have returned to Russia describe having had to pay their staffs out of their own bank accounts because federal funds were held up for half a year or more. Grant funding still has an ambiguous legal status. The federal programs to support R&D are not transparent, and the criteria often are vague. A plethora of administrative regulations limit the size of awards and the purposes for which funds may be used. Research projects are evaluated on the basis of their cost and length rather than the quality of such outputs as publications and patents.[60]

A host of restrictions limit flexibility in carrying out projects. Customs officials routinely delay the delivery of equipment, including basic necessities like petri dishes or reagents. Holding these supplies for half a year to extort bribes for releasing them may result in expiration of their useful life. Competitive bidding is rarely used in acquiring equipment. (Basic research and higher education [BRHE] did implement this, and the reaction of university administrators and researchers was astonishment.) The cost effectiveness of funds spent for R&D in Russia is about 10-15 percent of what it is in Europe or the United States.[61] In part, this is because administrators emphasize travel, equipment, and large infrastructure projects. These categories are the ones acceptable to the Ministry of Finance and are also the realms most susceptible to kickbacks, side payments, and other forms of corruption. Resistance to competition is thus both a professional and financial advantage.[62]

One way to encourage cost efficiency is by setting clear priorities. Russia consistently has too many priorities. One government study identified Russian priority sectors (to 2020) as: information and telecommunications, nanotechnology, life sciences, biotechnology, transportation and space; clean energy; security and counterterrorism; and advanced weapons. In November 2011, then President Medvedev identified five priority sectors: medical technology, energy and energy efficiency, information technology, space and space science, and telecommunictions.

Nanotechnology emerged as one of Putin's top priority programs. The reasons for this remain something of a mystery. In 2008, a group of physicists at one of our BRHE conferences joked that it is an Emperor's New Clothes analogy: when officials come to inspect results, the nano-products will be too small for them to see. While it is a major focus of science worldwide, nanotechnology does not play to Russia's traditional strengths. Much of the work in nanotechnology is done at the intersection of different disciplines: biotechnology and physics, biochemistry and medical devices, etc. The Soviet system "stovepiped" scientific work in individual disciplines, with research across disciplines being much harder to accomplish. Not only is Russia's effort dwarfed by U.S. spending, but China has a significant program that was introduced with little fanfare. In 2004-06, the United States was the clear leader in nanotechnology development, garnering 43 percent of world nanotechnology patents. China received 1 percent of the world's nanotech patents, to rank 13th; Russia, with less than one-half of 1 percent, ranked 22nd.[63]

China has developed a strikingly successful model of production innovation and reworking technology for the domestic market, while thus far doing little in new product innovation.[64] Beijing has been the focal point of the IT industry, a somewhat surprising development. In most countries, the high-technology corridor/center is not in the political capital. Adam Segal attributes Beijing's success to the relative weakness of the local government in the national capital. Not having the power to dominate technology businesses, the Beijing government adopted a relatively liberal approach to networks, while providing some financial support. Segal describes this as "the good mother-in-law" model.[65] Lacking the power to control standard operating environments (SOEs) or their spin-offs, the local officials established supportive, nonhierarchical relationships. Over time, Beijing's IT sector outperformed Shanghai, Xian, and Guangzhou, all regions with stronger production sectors.

Both Segal and Brenitz and Murprhee emphasize that China's indigenous companies learned from multinational corporations (MNCs) but focused their efforts on China's domestic market.[66] These studies also reinforce David Zweig's emphasis on the key role played by returnees. Recent analyses of MNCs in the two countries illustrate the differences in their approaches: Chinese firms have sought to learn and integrate; Russian firms focus on reaping profits, gaining control of enterprises in neighboring countries, and continuing to play by Russian rules at home.[67]

Why has Russia performed less well than China in reorienting a Soviet-style system from autarky to global competition? The existing literature provides a number of misleading answers:

- The Soviet system was overrated. This is correct but does not help us understand why some countries were able to overcome the obstacles more rapidly.
- Money. As we have seen, Russia now spends quite a bit on research, with surprisingly poor returns on the investment.
- The resource curse. Hydrocarbons create dangers of Dutch disease, crowd out domestic industry, and create excessive dependence on world prices for oil and gas. With the development of shale gas, hydrocarbon producers appear increasingly vulnerable to changes in technology. However, rather than precluding the diversification of an economy, income from natural resources should make it possible to

159

invest more in the diversification effort. When this fails to happen, it suggests that funds were either misallocated or misappropriated.

- Flawed privatization. The Russian variant of privatization was certainly a problem, but it did not preclude R&D.
- Poor policy advice. Russian officials generally blame the bad advice offered by foreigners for many of their difficulties. But countries like Poland, Slovenia, and Slovakia that implemented the foreign-designed programs more quickly and completely have achieved results that make it difficult to attribute Russia's economic performance to flawed policies forced upon them by foreign advisors. Failure to follow through with reforms on the part of "winners" is a more convincing explanation.
- "Mentality" is another favorite culprit: if only Russians thought differently, it would be possible to implement reforms more effectively. Again, the experience of other nations renders this argument questionable. It is hard to think of two nations with more "unique" orientations than Japan or China. Yet, both have managed to retain their unique attributes (everything seems to come with "Chinese characteristics") while participating in global economic and technological systems.
- A favorite explanation among Russian officials is that China's success represents the achievements of state programs implemented by an authoritarian regime. This explanation ignores the story of the first 2 decades of China's economic rise, when success came in sectors outside state control (technical and vocational

education and special economic zones with foreign investment). The SOEs were long the dead weight holding back economic development. It was only after major reforms in state enterprises in the late 1990s that some of them began to perform less poorly. Some continue to attribute their success to a continuing soft budget constraint, underwritten by state-owned banks.[68]

More promising answers focus on incentive structures and competition, epistemic communities, and institutions (including corruption). This is good news for Russia: None of these is a genetic trait or an irreversible condition. Rather, all of them can be altered by a package of wise government policies that offer adequate incentives, foster institutional development and competition, and punish malfeasance.

The truly important lessons from China are that embracing competition and globalization both reflects and reinforces economic and social interests. When reforms are successful, self-interested actors allied with supporters of reform oppose retrenchment. As Zweig emphasizes, the key is **partial** loss of control: the government has to be weakened/limited enough that it cannot be a major obstacle, while still retaining sufficient capacity to provide basic public goods like education, patent and Internet protocol protection, medical care, and security.[69]

Epistemic communities play a crucial role, but they must be encouraged to reform and to compete by a combination of incentives and sanctions: rewards for compliance, salary and career trajectory penalties for resistance. Peer pressure can help enormously in encouraging positive behavior patterns, with returnees in a position to play a unique role.[70] When scientists and educators have the option of receiving state subsidies and support, many find this preferable to competition in the free market.

The relationship between Russian academics and officials is complicated by an extreme variant of what might be called "the Scott Thompson factor."[71] Beginning in the Soviet era, it became common practice for government officials to receive academic credentials, and, in some instances, to gain election to the Academy of Sciences on dubious grounds. In the Putin era, about one-third of top Russian government officials hold *kandidat* of science or doctoral degrees that were purchased. Putin, Igor Sechin, and Viktor Zubkov all defended *kandidat* dissertations at the Mining Institute in St. Petersburg from 1997 to 1999. Some 18 pages of Putin's thesis, the core of his chapter on "Scientific Planning," were plagiarized from an economics textbook written by two University of Pittsburgh Business School professors and subsequently issued in a Russian translation by Mir publishing house.[72]

Following the wave of protests against Putin's return to the presidency and fraudulent elections, some observers thought there might be significant changes in the Russian political system. However, indications in the first months of Putin's third term as President make it difficult to be optimistic about reform. Putin has been weakened by the protests and the massive wave of satirical images produced by his opponents. Ironically, his weaker position may make it more difficult for him to introduce reforms that would be detrimental to Russian elites and epistemic communities. The changes promised in December have been skewed in ways that make them appear to have little impact: governors will be elected, but the choice of candidates will involve filters that preclude real opposition figures from running; rules for registering political parties have been relaxed, but in ways that are producing a plethora of competing parties that are likely to divide the opposition vote so that none of them reach the 5 percent threshold required for representation; nongovernmental organizations that receive foreign support will be required to register as foreign agents; and limits on the Internet, introduced as a way to preclude child pornography, open the door to censorship.

The protests have not ceased, though organizers did announce a pause for the summer. The next major demonstrations were scheduled for September 15, 2012. The mayoral, gubernatorial, and regional legislative elections in October were quite interesting. If plans to reduce subsidies for gas and other key commodities in July were carried through, higher heating costs will not be noticeable during the summer. By October, however, the higher payments would add economic issues to the political grievances of Putin's self-appointed candidacy and electoral fraud.

The changes that have been adopted for the electoral system thus far appear to be largely cosmetic. Restoring elections for governors removes the Kremlin's responsibility for both selecting and answering for the behavior of regional chief executives. At the same time, the process of approving candidates promises to guarantee that real opponents of United Russia will have a difficult time getting on the ballot.

Scientific research and innovation are not likely to experience a renaissance without more serious reform of educational and research institutions. The epistemic communities continue to resist reform, and a weakened government is not in a position to push them harder. Without greater social demand, and especially demand on the part of the academic community, the ongoing decline is likely to continue.

CONCLUSION

Return to the three questions posed by our conference organizers:

1. What must be done is diversification of the economy, which will generate demand and financial support for innovation. This also requires substantial changes to the political system (incentives, term limits, and feedback mechanisms); educational and research institutions (internationalize and foster competition); and epistemic communities (incentives and competition, which are preferable to sanctions).

2. What are the obstacles? Change is demonic, and therefore never easy. But beyond the common difficulties in altering any established system, in Russia, the most serious obstacles to accomplishing needed changes involve corruption and self-interest on the part of the agents involved. The problem is the winners, not the losers. China demonstrates that reorienting a Soviet-style system is challenging but not impossible. Russia demonstrates that, unless political leaders alter the incentive structures, epistemic communities will continue to do what they are used to doing.

3. What will be done, and with what consequences? Without a significant change in the signals and policies from the top, little will change. However, as long as oil rents supply adequate budget funding, a great deal of money will be spent. The most tragic result is that a large number of creative people will leave Russia. In terms of economic development and security issues, Russia will continue to be a declining power able

to influence global affairs primarily through negative rather than positive actions.

ENDNOTES - CHAPTER 4

1. At a conference at the Center for Strategic and International Studies (CSIS) in 2012, Alexei Kudrin cited the $130 figure. In a presentation at a fund-raising meeting at the Hermitage in June 2012, he cited a figure of $115, which corresponded to what President Putin and others had been giving at the St. Petersburg Economic Forum.

2. Richard McGregor, *The Party: The Secret World of China's Communist Rulers*, New York: Harper Collins, 2010; Ezra F. Vogel, *Deng Xiaoping and the Transformation of China*, Cambridge, MA, and London, UK: Harvard University Press, 2011; Kate Zhou, *China's Long March to Freedom: Grassroots Modernization*, New Burnswick, NJ, and London, UK: Transaction Publishers, 2009.

3. Edward L. Keenan, "Muscovite Political Folkways," *Russian Review,* Vol. 45, No. 2, April, 1986, pp. 115-181. Russian colleagues have pointed out that we probably know less about who makes decisions in the Putin system than we did in the Brezhnev era, when Central Committee assignments and Politburo responsibilities were relatively clear.

4. Barbara Geddes, "What Do We Know About Democratization after Twenty Years," *Annual Review of Political Science*, 1999, Vol. 2, pp. 115-144.

5. Andreas Schedler, "The Menu of Manipulation," *Journal of Democracy*, Vol. 13, No. 2, April 2002, pp. 36-50.

6. Steven Heydemann, "Upgrading Authoritarianism in the Arab World," Saban Center Analysis Paper, Washington, DC: Brookings Institution, 2007 available from *www.brookings.edu/papers/2007/10arabworld.aspx.*

7. W. Martin King Whyte, *The Myth of the Social Volcano,* Stanford, CA: Stanford University Press, 2010; Theresa Wright, *Accepting Authoritarianism: State-Society Relations in China's Reform Era,* Stanford, CA: Stanford University Press, 2010.

8. Jennifer Gandhi and Adam Przeworski, "Authoritarian Institutions and the Survival of Autocrats," *Comparative Political Studies*, Vol. 40, No. 11, 2007, pp. 1279-1301; Jennifer Gandhi, *Political Institutions Under Dictatorship*, New York: Cambridge University Press, 2008.

9. The recently completed doctoral dissertation by Leah Gilbert at Georgetown University provides detailed evidence of the effects of the crowding-out phenomenon. "State Mobilization Strategies and Political Competition in Hybrid Regimes," p. 2, Ph.D. Dissertation, Georgetown University, 2012.

10. Sidney Tarrow, "The Strategy of Paired Comparison: Toward a Theory of Practice," *Comparative Political Studies*, Vol. 43 No. 2, 2010, pp. 230-259.

11. Jonathan Unger, ed., *Associations and the Chinese State: Contested Spaces*, Armonk, NY: M. E. Sharpe, 2008; Richard Komaiko and Beibei Que, *Lawyers in Modern China*, Amherst, NY: Cambria Press, 2009; Harley Balzer, "Obuchenie Innovatsiiam v Rossii i v Kitae" ("Learning to Innovate in Russia and China"), *Pro et Contra*, Vol. 14, No. 3, May-June 2010, pp. 52-71.

12. David Shambaugh, *China's Communist Party: Atrophy and Adaptation*, Berkeley: University of California Press, 2008.

13. Gabriella Montinola, Yinyi Qian, and Barry R. Weingast, "Federalism, Chinese Style: The Political Basis for Economic Success in China," *World Politics*, Vol. 48, No. 1, October 1995, pp. 50-81; David Zweig, *Internationalizing China: Domestic Interests and Global Linkages*, Ithaca, NY, and London, UK: Cornell University Press, 2002.

14. Balzer, "Obuchenie Innovatsiiam."

15. Li Cheng, "China's Fifth Generation: Is Diversity a Source of Strength or Weakness?" *Asia Policy*, No. 6, July 2008, pp. 53-93.

16. *Ibid.*, and Shambaugh, *China's Communist Party*.

17. McGregor, *The Party: The Secret World of China's Communist Rulers.*

18. One of my Georgetown University colleagues presented his book to an audience at the Communist Party School in Beijing in 2012. The presentation provoked an animated discussion among the Chinese analysts about both the imperative for reform and the difficulty of combating entrenched interests.

19. Mäkinen Sirke, "Surkovian Narrative on the Future of Russia: Making Russia a World Leader," *Journal of Communst Studies and Transition Politics,*" Vol. 27, No. 2, 2011, pp. 143-165.

20. Harley Balzer, "Managed Pluralism: Vladimir Putin's Emerging Regime," *Post-Soviet Affairs,* Vol. 19, No. 3, July-August-September 2003, pp. 189-226.

21. Some of the best documentation of concerns among the Russian elite has come from Mikhail Dmitriev's Center for Strategic Development. Three reports have documented growing unease with Russia's economic and political trajectory. The most recent is Center for Strategic Development, "Obshchestvo i vlast' v usloviiakh politicheskogo krizisa. Doklad ekspertov TsCR Komitetu grazhdanskikh initsiativ" ("Society and Power in Conditions of Crisis: Report of the Experts at the Center for Strategic Development for The Committee for Civic Initiative"), Moscow, Russia: May 2012. Also see Mikhail Dmitriev and Daniel Treisman, "The Other Russia: Discontent Grows in the Hinterlands, *Foreign Affairs,* Vol. 91, No. 5, September/October 2012. Also see Alexei Kudrin and O. Sergienko, "Posledstviia Krizisa i Perspektivy Sotsialno-Ekonomicheskogo Razvitiia Rossii" ("Consequences of the Crisis and Perspective For the Social-Economic Development of Russia"), *Voprosy Ekonomiki,* No. 3, 2011, pp. 4-19.

22. INSOR, *Obretenie Budushchego. Strategiia 2012 (Acquiring the Future: Strategy 2012),* Moscow, Russia: Institut Sovremennogo Razivtiia (Institute for Contemporary Development) 2011, available from *www.insor-russia.ru/files/Finding_of_the_Future*; Sergei Balanovskii and Mikhail Dmitriev, *Politicheskii Krizis v Rossii i Vozmozhnye Mekhanizmy Ego Razvitiia (The Political Crisis in Russia and Possible Mechanisms for its Development),* Washington, DC: Center for Strategic Development, 2011; V. Milov, B. Nemtsov,

V. Ryzhkov, and O. Shorina, eds., X *Putin. Korruptiia. Nezavisimi ekspertnyi doklad* (*Putin. Corruption. Independent Ekspert Report*), Moscow, Russia: Partiia Narodnoi Svodody, 2011, available from *www.putin-itogi.ru/f/Putin-i-korruptsiya-doklad.pdf.*

23. Lilia Shevtsova, "Putinism Under Siege: Implosion, Atrophy or Revolution?" *Journal of Democracy*, Vol. 23, No. 3, July 2012, pp. 19-32.

24. Michael McFaul, "The Fourth Wave of Democracy *and* Dictatorship: Noncooperative Transitions in the Postcommunist World," *World Politics*, Vol. 54, No. 2, January 2002, pp. 212-244.

25. Henry E. Hale, Michael McFaul, and Timothy J. Colton, "Putin and the 'Delegative Democracy' Trap: Evidence from Russia's 2003-04 Elections," *Post-Soviet Affairs*, Vol. 20, No. 4, October-December 2004, pp. 285-319.

26. Derek S. Hutcheson, "Protest and Disengagement in the Russian Federal Elections of 2003-04," *Perspectives on European Politics and Society*, Vol. 5, No. 2, 2004, pp. 305-330.

27. Alfred B. Evans, Jr., "The Framing of Discontent by Protest Movements in Russia," Paper Presented at the Association for Slavic, East European, and Eurasian Studies (ASEEES) National Convention, November 17-20, 2011.

28. See Endnote 22. All of the reports are available from *www.csr.ru.*

29. ZN. V. Zubarevich, *Sotsial'noe razvitie regionov Rossii: Problemy I Tendentsii Perekhodnogo Perioda* (*Social Development of Russian Regions: Problems and Tendencies in the Transition Period*), Moscow, Russia: Knizhnyy dom "Librokom," 2012; and Natalia Zubarevich, "Four Russias: Rethinking the Post-Soviet Map," March 29, 2012, available from *www.opendemocracy.net.*

30. In the Chernogolovka Mayoral election, physicist Vladimir Razumov won a majority. The result was overturned; but following protests, this was reversed, and the officials responsible for rejecting the results were dismissed. In Yaroslavl, Yevgeny Urshalov, a candidate running in opposition to United Russia,

won with 70 percent of the vote. In Astrakhan, opposition candidate Oleg Shein staged a hunger strike to protest the falsification of election results. Ombudsman Lukin and other Moscow figures expressed support. In Togliatti, Sergei Andreev, known as a liberal, defeated the United Russia candidate General Alexander Shakhov.

31. June 4, 2012, available from *www.opendemocracy.net.*

32. These topics are discussed in Harley Balzer, "Russia and the Limits of Authoritarian Resilience," Richard Weitz, ed., *Can We Manage a Declining Russia?* Washington, DC: Hudson Institute, November 2011, pp. 85-116.

33. At the June 12, 2012, celebration of Russia's National Day at the Russian Embassy in Washington, Ambassador Kislyak repeated the claim that Russia has overcome its demographic decline. Author's personal observation.

34. Thomas P. Bernstein and Hua-Yu Li, eds., *China Learns from the Soviet Union, 1949-Present*, Lanham, MD: Lexington Books, 2010.

35. Harley Balzer, "Russia and China in the Global Economy," *Demokratizatsiya,* Vol. 16, No. 1, Winter 2008, pp. 37-48. For a good summary of Russian views of globalization, see Andrei P. Tsygankov, "Globalization: A Russian Perspective," Arlene B. Tickner and David L Blaney, eds., *Thinking International Relations Differently*, London, UK: Routledge, 2012, pp. 205-217. Lilia Shevtsova has suggested that members of the Russia elite globalize quite readily in their personal lives, sending their children abroad to study, purchasing real estate, and keeping money in foreign bank accounts. But they do not fully integrate. See Bobo Lo and Lilia Shevtsova, *A 21st Century Myth – Authoritarian Modernization in Russia and China*, Moscow, Russia: Carnegie Moscow Center, 2012.

36. This section draws on Harley Balzer, "Obuchenie innovatsiiam v Rossii i v Kitae" ("Learning to Innovate in Russia and China"), *Pro et Contra*, Vol. 14, No. 3, May-June 2010, pp. 52-71.

37. The "excess" of higher education enrollees over high school graduates consists primarily of students who attended secondary specialized institutions and then sought higher education.

38. Balzer, "Obuchenie innovatsiiam"; Igor Fediukin and Isak Frumin, "Rossiiskie VUZy-Flagmeny" ("Russian Flagship Higher Education Institutions"), *Pro et Contra*, Vol. 14, No. 3, May-June 2010, pp. 19-31.

39. From 1998 to 2009, the author was a member of the Governing Council for the Basic Research and Higher Education Program funded by the John D. and Catherine T. MacArthur Foundation, the Carnegie Corporation of New York, and the Russian Ministry of Education and Science. The program established 16 research and education centers at universities across Russia. In each of the four rounds of competition, our Russian colleagues from the Ministry expressed serious concerns about issues of regional distribution.

40. See *www.timeshighereducation.co.uk/world-university-rankings*. Other rankings have been kinder to Russian institutions. The Shanghai Jiao Tong Top 100 put Moscow University in 77th place in 2009, but dropped it to 80 in 2012. St. Petersburg fell to a tie with 99 other institutions for 401-500. Information available from *www.shanghairanking.com*.

41. In the most recent Shanghai Jiao Tong rankings, for 2011, Moscow University had dropped to 80 from 75 in 2009. St. Petersburg University was in a tie for 401-500. No other Russian institutions made the top 500. In mathematics, Moscow University ranked 35 in 2011, down from 23 in 2009. Information available from *www.shanghairanking.com*. As many expected, Chinese institutions showed substantial progress. Four Chinese institutions were in the 50-way tie for 151-200 (Peiking, Shanghai Jiao Tong, Tsinghua, and Zhejiang). Three Chinese universities were in the tie for 201-300; seven for rank 301-400, and 14 among the 100 ranking 401-500. That placed 28 Chinese institutions in the top 500. Somewhat astonishingly, Hong Kong institutions fare almost as poorly as do Russian universities: Two are tied for 151-200, and three more are in the group at 201-300. Whereas *The Times* rankings of Russian institutions are similar to the Shanghai Jiao Tong numbers, *The Times* ranks Hong Kong universities and institutes far higher.

42. The Institute of International Education in New York publishes annual figures on the numbers of foreign students. Information available from *www.iie.org/*.

43. David Zweig and Donglin Han, "'Sea Turtles' or 'Seaweed'? The Employment of Overseas Returnees in China," France/ILO Symposium, Paris, France, May 2008.

44. Koen Jonkers, *Mobility, Migration and the Chinese Scientific Research System*, Abington, UK: Routledge, 2010.

45. Dan Breznitz and Michael Murphree, *The Run of the Red Queen: Government, Innovation, Globlization, and Economic Growth in China*, New Haven, CT, and London, UK: Yale University Press, 2011.

46. T. L. Kliachko, "Main Tendencies of the System of Education of the Russian Federation in 2007," *Russian Education and Society*, Vol. 51, No. 7, July 2009, pp. 35-57.

47. N. V. Popravko and A. Iu. Rykun, *Stanovlenie i Razvitie Rynka Dopolnitel'nykh Obrazovatel'nykh Uslug na Territorii Tomskogo Regiona. Analiz Povedeniia Potrebitelei. (Creation and Development of the Market for Supplementary Educational Services in the Tomsk Region. Analysis of Consumer Behavior)*, Tomsk, Russia: Izdatelstvo Tomskogo Nniversiteta, 2002.

48. Georgii Satarov, *Diagnostika Rossiiskoi korruptsii: Sotsiologicheskii Analiz (Otchet Podgotovlen Fondom INDEM (Disgnostics of Russian Corruption: A Sociological Analysis — A Report Prepared by the INDEM Foundation)*, Moscow, Russia: May 2002; Popravko and Rykun.

49. In the United States, the response to a much less dramatic demographic shift was to seek a greater number of nontraditional students. While this is possible in Russia, it does not appear likely that the numbers would be adequate. Russia already enrolls nearly 5 percent of the population in higher education, and as the population ages and the number of high school graduates declines, the pressure to augment the labor force will be enormous. Harley Balzer, "Demography and Democracy in Russia: Human Capi-

171

tal Challenges to Democratic Consolidation," *Demokratizatsiya*, Vol. 11, No. 1, Winter 2003, pp. 95-109.

50. For more detail on this reversal, see Balzer, "Obuchenie innovatsiiam." An English translation is available as Mortara Working Paper 2011-17, from *www12.georgetown.edu/sfs/docs/mwp_2011_17.pdf*.

51. Soviet success was mainly in theoretical fields that required little experimental work, though, of course, there were exceptions in nuclear research, biological weapons, and some other military-related specialties. See Thane Gustafson, "Why Doesn't Soviet Science Do Better than it Does?" Linda Lubrano and Susan Gross Solomon, eds., *The Social Context of Soviet Science*, Boulder, CO: Westview Press, 1980; and Harley Balzer, *Soviet Science on the Edge of Reform*, Boulder, CO: Westview Press 1989.

52. Richard Connolly, "Climbing the Ladder? High-Technology Export Performance in Emerging Europe," *Eurasian Geography and Economics*, Vol. 53, No. 3, 2012, pp. 356-379.

53. Balzer, "Obuchenie innovatsiiam.'

54. Asif Siddiqi, *The Red Rockets' Glare: Spaceflight and the Soviet Imagination, 1857-1957*, Cambridge, MA, and New York: Cambridge University Press, 2010. Siddiqi shows that there was no Soviet program to launch a satellite until after Joseph Stalin's death. The interest in space was kept alive by Sergei Korolev and other fanatics. Korolev finally was given the chance to strap together a bunch of relatively simple booster rockets to launch the first Sputnik.

55. Balzer, *Soviet Science on the Edge of Reform*.

56. Gavin Wright and Jesse Czelusta, "Mineral Resources and Economic Development," MS Paper, Stanford, CA: Stanford University, October 2003.

57. The journal *EKO*, No. 1, 2002, published a set of articles on innovation in the Tatarstan oil industry. For Putin's views, see Harley Balzer, "Vladimir Putin's Academic Writings and Russian Natural Resource Policy," *Problems of Post-Communism*, Vol. 53, No. 1, January-February 2006, pp. 48-54.

58. Alexey Prazdnichnykh and Kari Liuhto, "Can Russian companies innovate? Views of some 250 Russian CEOs," Turku, Finland: Electronic Publications of Pan-European Institute No. 21, 2010; Irina Dezhina, "Na Lifte, Chrez Platformu—v Klaster: Soedinit' Biznes I Nauku—Poka Nerazreshimaia problema v Rossii" ("On the Elevator, Across the Platform—To the Cluster: Bringing Together Business and Science—Thus Far an Unresolved Problem in Russia"), *Nezavisimaia gazeta*, April 25, 2012.

59. Irina G. Dezhina, "Otsenka Mer Gosudarstevnnoi Politiki Rossii Oblasti Nauki" ("Evaluating Measures of State Policy in the Sphere of Science"), *EKO*, No. 2, 2012, pp. 145-163.

60. These comments have been collected by the author from multiple visits to Russian universities and from the annual conferences convened by the basic research and higher education (BRHE) program.

61. Dezhina, "Evaluating Measures of State Policy in the Sphere of Science."

62. In 2010, Alexander Blankov of the Interior Ministry Department of Economic Security estimated corruption in Russian education to total $5.5 Billion. Some $1.5 billion was spent on the admission process. (*Itar-Tass*, May 25, 2010). The same day, *Itar-Tass* quoted Viktor Panin of the Russian society for the protection of rights of educational services consumers on the prices for specific educational credentials: Secondary school certificates cost $500; VUZ diplomas cost $700-$1,000; Kandidat degrees are priced at $20,000 to $50,000, while Nauk credentials cost $30,000 to $70,000. Panin estimates that about 5,000 Nauk credentials are sold annually.

63. Balzer, "Obuchenie innovatsiiam."

64. Harley Balzer, "Russia and China in the Global Economy," pp. 37-48; Breznits and Murphree, *The Run of the Red Queen*.

65. Adam Segal, *Digital Dragon: High-Technology Enterprises in China*, Ithaca, NY, and London, UK: Cornell University Press, 2003.

66. Segal, *Digital Dragon*; Breznitz and Murphree, *The Run of the Red Queen*; also see Zhou Yu *The Inside Story of China's High-Tech Industry: Making Silicon Valley in Beijing*, Lanham, MD: Rowman & Littlefield, 2008.

67. Andrei Panibratov, *Russian Multinationals: From Regional Supremacy to Global Lead*, London, UK, and New York: Routledge Contemporary Russia and Eastern Europe Series, 2012; Jean-Paul, Larcon, ed., *Chinese Multinationals*, Singapore and Hackensack, NJ: World Scientific, 2009.

68. Huang Yasheng, *Capitalism with Chinese Characteristics: Entrepreneurship and the State*, Cambridge and London, UK: Cambridge University Press, 2008.

69. Zweig, *Internationalizing China*.

70. David Zweig, "Returnees, Technology Transfer, and China's Economic Development," Hong Kong University of Science and Technology, Center on China's Transnational Relations, Working Paper No. 28, presented June 2009; David Zweig, Chung Siu Fung, and Wilfried Vanhonacker, "Rewards of Technology: Explaining China's Reverse Migration," Center on China's Transnational Relations, Working Paper No. 11, The Hong Kong University of Science and Technology, September 2006.

71. Scott Thompson, the CEO of Yahoo, was forced to resign in May 2012 when it became known that he had "padded" his resume. For many years, Thompson had claimed that his undergraduate degree was in both accounting and computer science, when it was only in accounting.

72. Harley Balzer, "The Putin Thesis and Russian Energy Policy," *Post-Soviet Affairs*, Vol. 21, No. 3, 2005, pp. 210-225; Allison M. Heinrichs, "Putin Plagiarized from Pitt Professors," *Pittsburgh Tribune-Review*, March 28, 2006.

CHAPTER 5

RUSSIA AS A POLE OF POWER:
PUTIN'S REGIONAL INTEGRATION AGENDA

Janusz Bugajski

With the return of Vladimir Putin to Russia's Presidency, the Kremlin is reinvigorating its regional assertiveness, and several former Soviet republics are under increasing pressure to participate in Moscow's integrationist initiatives. No longer a credible global superpower, Russia aims to become the preeminent Eurasian power and not simply a junior partner of the United States or any other large state. Even before his re-election in March 2012, Putin underscored the Kremlin's ambitions in Russia's immediate neighborhood and outlined the concept of a Russian-led Eurasian Union (EurU) that will evidently remain central in his efforts to forge a legacy as a gatherer of post-Soviet lands.[1]

Among the top priorities that Putin set for his third presidential term is the reintegration of the former Soviet republics, based on tighter economic links and culminating in a political and security pact with Russia at its center. Moscow is evidently fearful lest the territory of the former Soviet Union permanently divides and drifts into European and Asian "spheres of influence."[2] Hence, Putin seeks to create a new Eurasian bloc that will balance the European Union (EU) in the West and China in the East. Economic linkages will create political ties and mesh with interstate security structures, thus making it less likely that Russia's neighbors can join alternative military, economic, and political alliances. Russia would thereby be able to strengthen its geopolitical position as a "pole of power" in a multipolar world.

To achieve its grand ambitions, Moscow needs to assemble around itself a cluster of states that are loyal or subservient to Russian interests, and it has been encouraged in this endeavor by several favorable developments in recent years. First, as a by-product of President Barack Obama's administration "reset" policy toward Moscow launched in early 2009, Washington has curtailed, if not completely discarded, its campaign to enlarge the North Atlantic Treaty Organization (NATO) and secure the post-Soviet neighborhood within Western structures. This has left the East European states bordering Russia more exposed and vulnerable to Moscow's pressures and integrationist maneuvers. Moreover, Belarus, Moldova, and Ukraine are not priority interests for the current American administration, whether in terms of democratic development, national sovereignty, or their strategic location.

Second, the financial crunch, economic downturns, and political stresses within the EU have diminished Brussels, Belgium's outreach toward the post-Soviet countries. This has decreased the momentum of the EU's Eastern Partnership (EaP), an initiative launched in May 2009 and designed to harmonize the European post-Soviet states with EU standards. Moscow has concluded that the EU is in serious disarray and decline and will be preoccupied with its internal problems for several years, if, indeed, it does not actually fracture.

Third, there is visible disillusionment with the EU in many of the post-Soviet capitals. They do not possess the roadmap, direction, or commitment to full integration with the West, unlike the vision and promise that was given to the Central Europeans after they liberated themselves from Moscow in the early 1990s or to the Western Balkan countries through the EU's Stabilization and Association Agreements after the collapse of Yugoslavia. Conversely, in the case of Belarus and Ukraine, there is tangible frustration in several EU capitals over their ongoing political regression, human rights abuses, and stilted economic reforms.

Fourth, the return of Vladimir Putin to the Kremlin is re-energizing Russia's neoimperial ambitions through such comprehensive geostrategic objectives as the formation of a EurU. As an added bonus, an assertive foreign policy helps distract attention from domestic opposition and the convulsions inside the Russian Federation. Putin's renewed presidency has been presented as vital to Russia's national security in two ways. It will allegedly protect Russia from internal turmoil generated by disruptive public protests, and it can rebuild Eurasia under Russia's management and remove unwanted Western influences that purportedly challenge the security of the Russian Federation.

MULTIPOLAR GOALS

A principal objective of Moscow's foreign policy is to restore Russia as a major regional power.[3] In this equation, the Kremlin's overarching goal toward the West is to reverse U.S. global predominance by transforming "unipolarity" into "multipolarity," in which Russia exerts increasing international leverage through its Eurasian centrality. Kremlin officials believe that the world should be organized around a new global version of the 19th century "Concert of Europe" in which great powers balance their interests and smaller countries orbit around them, essentially as satellites or dependencies. Moscow favors multipolarity over multilateralism. In the latter, its voice becomes diluted in various multinational formats; in the former, its role is raised as an important global player.

Moscow's "multipolar" concept is based on two geopolitical premises—the decline of the United States and the emergence of new "poles" or centers of international power, among which Russia becomes a significant player. Conventional wisdom presupposes that the world has entered the era of multipolarity, in which regional influence is maintained by a few select powers. In reality, the future will be much more irregular and unpredictable. There are at least three conceptual problems with the notion of multipolarity. First, it assumes that a large country has substantial attractive influence to become a legitimate magnetic force vis-à-vis its neighbors. Instead, an ambitious government may simply cajole and pressure its neighbors to grudgingly recognize its temporary dominance. However, such a pole of power will generate little loyalty; on the contrary, it may become inherently unstable by increasing regional resentments and stoking interstate tensions. Russia presents a stark example of such a destabilizing pole of power aspiring to regional dominance.

Second, the concept of multipolarity underestimates the interests and aspirations of smaller and medium-sized countries by placing them within the confines of the ambitions of larger regional powers. It can thereby be used as a smokescreen and even a justification for neoimperial dominance that places limitations on the national independence of numerous subordinated states, including Ukraine, Belarus, and Moldova.

Third, nonpolarity, the converse of multipolarity, does not automatically presuppose international chaos as the multipolar proponents claim. The idea of chaos assumes that we would witness a life and death struggle for survival between and within competing states. Although this could be the case in some specific regions, such as parts of the Middle East or Central Africa, the self-appointed polar powers may themselves be the source of conflict, either with each other or by following a policy of "divide and rule" toward their numerous neighbors.

In other regions, the absence of a regional hegemon could actually encourage countries to cooperate around common interests to avoid both chaos and outside dominance. As a result, instead of ensuring stability and security, the struggle for multipolarity can itself engender conflict, especially where two or more powers compete for predominant influence, while smaller states resist their pressures or actively seek to embroil them in conflicts in order to gain various national advantages. More than likely, over the coming decade, we will witness a mixed picture of polarities. The United States will remain the single strongest power but is not capable of always acting unilaterally or deploying its forces globally. Meanwhile, several multipolar aspirants will compete for regional influence with varying degrees of success in attracting neighbors into their orbit.

In seeking to more rapidly diminish American power, Russia's leaders support the creation of a "counter-hegemonic bloc."[4] This is a modernized version of the anti-American or anti-Western alliance that was pursued by the Soviet Union throughout the Cold War and ultimately failed. As the Russian case has demonstrated, expressions of strategic opposition to the West are driven largely by political leaders fearful of losing domestic power and international influence. However, no constructive or all-encompassing ideology has emerged that can unite and mobilize disparate states, which often possess contrary ambitions in overlapping regions. Moreover, such a strategy faces three core problems: it will stimulate new conflicts with the West, including the EU and NATO; it is unlikely to lead to meaningful or durable cooperation between such diverse countries and competitors as China, India, and Russia; and it will be resisted by states and governments that either aspire to be part of the West, look to the West for protection, or admire the liberal democratic model.

Future geopolitical configurations will not be neatly "multipolar," a concept that Moscow supports as it divides the world into regions where specific countries dominate and their influence is considered legitimate. Much more likely, we will witness a continuing struggle for zones of influence by larger states, together with resistance by smaller powers against subservience to larger and assertive neighbors. In sum, any theory of international relations, such as the multipolar concept, needs to account for a complex and changeable reality; if it cannot explain that reality, then it should be defined primarily as a tool of foreign policy pursued by particular capitals.

INTERESTS, AMBITIONS, AND STRATEGIES

In assessing Putin's integrationist agenda, it is useful to distinguish between Russia's realistic national interests and its grander state ambitions. For instance, Moscow's security is not challenged by the NATO accession of neighboring states. However, its ability to control the security and foreign policy orientations of its post-Soviet neighbors is certainly undermined by their accession to NATO and through allied protection of their national independence.

While its goals are imperial through its multipolar orientation, Kremlin strategies are pragmatic, and its tactics are elastic. The authorities employ flexible methods, including enticements, threats, incentives, and pressures, where Russia's national ambitions are seen as predominating over those of neighbors. Moscow engages in asymmetric offensives by injecting itself in neighbor's decisionmaking, capturing important sectors of local economies, subverting vulnerable political systems, and corrupting or discrediting national leaders. Russia's neoimperial project no longer relies on Soviet-era instruments, such as ideological allegiance, military control, or the implanting of proxy governments. Instead, the primary goal is to exert predominant influence over the foreign and security policies of immediate neighbors so they will either remain neutral or support Russia's international agenda.

The word "pragmatic" has been loosely applied in describing Russia's foreign policy by implying moderation and cooperation, and by counterposing it to an ideologized imperial policy characteristic of the Cold War. Paradoxically, "pragmatic imperialism" is a useful way to describe Russia's foreign policy, particularly in the strategies and tactics employed to realize specific state ambitions. These ambitions are twofold with regard to Russia's neighbors: foreign policy subservience to Russia and integration in Moscow-directed security and economic organizations. The major multinational organizations promoted by Moscow to enhance integration and centralization include the Commonwealth of Independent States (CIS), the Collective Security Treaty Organization (CSTO), the Eurasian Economic Community (EEC), the Customs

Union (CU), the Common Economic Space (CES), and the recently announced EurU.[5]

Created in December 1991, the CIS has had limited impact, and several former republics joined primarily to ensure Moscow's economic assistance or, in the case of Armenia, permanent military protection. Several post-Soviet countries have maintained their distance from Russia despite their CIS membership. Ukraine, Moldova, Georgia, and Azerbaijan are focused on maintaining their independence and have viewed the CIS as a potential threat. Georgia joined the CIS in 1993 and left in August 2008 after its short war with Russia. Uzbekistan maintains a distance from Russia, although it joined the EEC and the CSTO briefly between 2006 and 2008, while Turkmenistan has been fully isolationist. Ukraine and Turkmenistan never ratified the CIS statutes and consider themselves only observers or participants.

The CSTO, a military alliance that includes Armenia, Belarus, Kazakhstan, Kyrgyzstan, Russia, Tajikistan, and Uzbekistan, is designed to counter NATO aspirations in Eurasia. Its main charters are currently being revised, specifically in the arena of decision-making, for possible deployments.[6] The current charter requires unanimity to pass a decision, but under the planned revisions, only states with an interest in a given decision would be allowed a vote, thus curtailing any potential opposition to Kremlin policy in case a military mission is deemed necessary by Moscow.

The EEC was created in October 2000 at a summit in Astana, Kazakhstan, from the prior CU and is viewed in Moscow as a stepping-stone toward the proposed EurU. It includes Russia, Belarus, Kazakhstan, Kyrgyzstan, Tajikistan, and Uzbekistan. In July 2011, Russia, Belarus, and Kazakhstan launched a CU to remove all trade barriers between the three states. In practice, Belarus and Kazakhstan have been forced to adopt the higher Russian import tariffs, and both capitals have demanded direct payments from Russia as compensation. Joining the Russia-focused CU may also preclude involvement in a free trade zone with the EU for the East European countries.

In October 2011, Putin hosted a meeting of prime ministers from Armenia, Belarus, Kazakhstan, Kyrgyzstan, Moldova, Tajikistan, and Ukraine in St. Petersburg and announced an agreement to form a free trade zone after years of fruitless negotiations. On January 1, 2012, a formal agreement was signed to create the CES, an undivided common market embracing the three CU economies, together with Ukraine and open to other post-Soviet countries. On the eve of accession to the CES, the Presidents of Belarus, Russia, and Kazakhstan also signed the Declaration of Eurasian Economic Integration. President Dmitry Medvedev invited all other EEC members to join the CES, including the three EEC observer states of Armenia, Moldova, and Ukraine.

Business entities of the three CES countries are guaranteed freedom of movement of goods, services, capital, and labor. Thus far, Kiev has resisted these enticements, fearful that they would subvert Ukrainian sovereignty. All these plans called for the ultimate establishment of a euro-like single currency system. The transition to the EurU has been described as the final goal of economic integration. It envisaged a free trade regime; unified customs and nontariff regulation measures; common access to internal markets; a unified transportation system; a common energy market; and a single currency. The Moscow summit of the EEC on March 19, 2012, charted a detailed integration strategy, with a view to having the EEC reshaped into a fully-fledged economic union by 2015.[7] These integrative economic measures would also become undergirded by a tighter political alliance.

Within the first 2 weeks of his renewed presidency in May 2012, Putin hosted an informal CIS summit with most of the former Soviet states, as well as a CSTO extraordinary session with Armenia, Belarus, Kazakhstan, Kyrgyzstan, Tajikistan, and Uzbekistan. In all these meetings, the goal of the EurU has featured prominently. Putin's notion of a EurU is of a powerful supranational association capable of becoming one of the poles in the modern world and of serving as an efficient bridge between Europe and the dynamic Asia-Pacific region.[8]

Putin believes that the EurU should be built on the inheritance of the Soviet Union, including: infrastructure, a developed system of regional production specialization, and a common space of language, science, and culture.

How successful any of these integrationist projects will prove in practice remains debatable. For instance, some analysts believe that the EurU is likely to be costly and unsuccessful and will result in trade disruption.[9] Nevertheless, the pursuit of supranational integration is itself damaging to the security and independence of states neighboring the Russian Federation, as they will be prevented from fully expressing their sovereignty by freely choosing their international alliances. In calculating the impact of Russia's pressure politics revolving around its integrationist projects, it is useful to examine in more detail Moscow's policies toward its immediate European targets—Ukraine, Belarus, and Moldova—and then to assess the impact on the broader Central-Eastern European region.

TARGET UKRAINE

Few Russian politicians accept the permanent independence of Ukraine, a country viewed as the historic origin of Russian statehood.[10] Russian elites deny Ukraine a separate history and view its national independence as a temporary aberration. Their ideal scenario for Ukraine is a close political, economic, and military alliance. The internal characteristics of the Ukrainian government have been of lesser interest as long as Kiev follows Russia's foreign and security policies and does not succeed in gaining NATO membership.

Throughout the January 2010 presidential election campaign in Ukraine, the Kremlin did not overtly favor any specific candidate in case the candidate was defeated. It also calculated that growing public frustration with political infighting would lead to disillusionment with liberal democracy and growing support for a more authoritarian leader close to Moscow. Indeed, Ukrainian citizens became increasingly embittered with the results of the 2004 Orange Revolution, particularly with the political battles between former Orange coalition partners and subsequently elected Victor Yanukovych, the anti-Orange leader, as President.

Although Ukraine was one of the founding members of the CIS, which was styled as a loose multinational association among the newly independent states, it raised reservations on issues such as a single currency, military affairs, and foreign policy in order to prevent the new structure from becoming a Soviet replica. Kiev proved successful in thwarting Kremlin designs to construct a unified economic and security policy. However, power struggles between political interest groups and industrial lobbies in Ukraine have provided ample opportunities for Moscow to pursue its agenda of reintegration.

In order to return Kiev more firmly under its control, Moscow has engaged in various forms of pressure and subterfuge. These include energy blackmail, economic buyouts, media propaganda, the discrediting of pro-Western politicians, the manipulation of ethnic and regional grievances, and lingering territorial claims. Russia's new military doctrine also bestows Moscow with the right to intervene in neighboring states containing large Russian populations.

The Russian or Russophone minority, constituting about a third of the Ukrainian population, has been exploited by Moscow to apply political pressures on Kiev. Russian officials have demanded dual citizenship for co-ethnics in Ukraine and initially used this as a pretext to delay signing a bilateral state treaty. Kiev rejected such proposals, as they would allow Moscow to claim informal jurisdiction over regions where Russian-speakers predominated. Moscow also raised the specter of creeping "Ukrainianization" allegedly directed against Russian ethnics, implying attempts by West Ukrainian nationalists to oust the Russian language from official communications, thwart Russian cultural influences, and limit the role of the Russian Orthodox Church.

Moscow registered success in its external language policy on June 5, 2012, when Ukraine's parliament approved, in a preliminary reading, a law that would allow the use of Russian as a second official language in 11 Ukrainian regions where over 10 percent of inhabitants use Russian as their first language, together with the cities of Kiev and Sevastopol.[11] The law needs to be approved in two more readings and signed by President Yanukovych to take effect. The governing Party of Regions sought to consolidate its voting base among Russian speakers before the October 2012 parliamentary elections and succumbed to persistent pressures from Moscow. Once approved, the "regional language" law will affect schooling and citizens' interactions with local authorities. Observers fear that it will discourage Russian-speakers from learning the official state language and decrease their loyalty to the Ukrainian state. It could also increase ethnic tensions and aggravate social and regional divisions.[12]

Kiev remains concerned about possible Kremlin support for separatism on the Crimean Peninsula and in eastern areas of the country. Until now, it has not served Russia's interests to provoke a full-scale separatist conflict, as this would have a destabilizing impact along Russia's borders. However, the Crimean issue has been manipulated by Russian nationalists to prevent the Ukrainian government from moving in a pro-Western direction. Officials repeatedly refer to Crimea as "ancient Russian land." This autonomous region remains a potential flashpoint of separatism if relations between Ukraine and Russia seriously deteriorate.

Control over Ukraine's internal security is also an important component of Russia's oversight. In March 2012, President Yanukovych agreed to the introduction of Russian advisers in the Security Service (SBU) and joint consultation with Moscow over future government appointments.[13] Russian influence over Ukraine's security forces is evident in the appointment of Russian citizens Igor Kalinin and Dmitri Salamatin as SBU Chairman and Minister of Defense, respectively. Kalinin maintains close ties to Russia and headed the Directorate on State Protection (UDO), the former Soviet KGB 9th Directorate. His appointment will also lead to enhanced cooperation between the SBU and Federal Security Service (FSB).

Energy supplies have been persistently manipulated as economic tools of Russian policy. Ukraine depends on Russia for more than 70 percent of its oil and gas needs and is heavily indebted to Russia's energy monopolies. Moscow's ability to injure Ukraine's economy through energy blackmail, the raising of prices, or calling in debts challenges the country's independence. Russia has periodically engaged in "energy wars" with Ukraine, during which cuts in energy deliveries crippled sizable parts of the economy. The gas war of 2005-06 highlighted the use of energy to apply political pressure on a government seeking to move permanently out of Russia's orbit.

Moscow has focused on acquiring Ukraine's energy infrastructure, as this ties the country into state-controlled Russian interests. Gazprom has sought a majority stake in pipelines crossing Ukraine. Its schemes were initially blocked, as the Ukrainian parliament prohibited the privatization of the oil and gas industries. Prime Minister Putin pushed for a merger between Gazprom and Naftogaz of Ukraine. Naftogaz controls the natural gas system and retail market in Ukraine. Russia uses the pipeline network to transport about 80 percent of its gas to the EU, or approximately 20 percent of the EU's total gas needs. Although Kiev may resist a full Gazprom takeover of Naftogaz pipelines and storage facilities, it could eventually accede to a joint venture between the two companies.[14]

Russia and Ukraine are also embroiled in a dispute over the price and volume of Russian gas. Kiev insists the current price is too high and wants to renegotiate the 2009 gas deal, while Moscow is pushing for control of Ukraine's gas transit system to Europe as part of a deal to cut prices.[15] Three elements of the agreement are problematic: the price Ukraine pays for gas, the volume of Russian gas that Ukraine is obliged to buy annually, and the fee Russia pays to use Ukraine's gas transit system.[16] Kiev feels that the first two figures should decrease dramatically, while the third should increase. At over $400 per thousand cubic meters, Ukraine pays one of the highest prices for Russian gas in Europe, while the transit fees Russia pays to Ukraine are low in comparison to other transit countries.

Moscow has supported and exploited political disputes in leaders, as they weaken Kiev's Western aspirations and reinforce "Ukraine fatigue" in the West. The election victory of Viktor Yanukovych in February 2010 signaled that Ukraine remained divided on the question of Western integration as the new President favored state neutrality. On July 1, 2010, Ukraine's parliament ratified a new law on "The Fundamentals of Domestic and Foreign Policy" that dropped the goal of acquiring NATO membership. This has also suited several NATO and EU leaders who remain hesitant in bringing Ukraine into either organization.

Moscow has induced Kiev to integrate more closely with Russia and into its multinational formats. In April 2010, a new deal was signed by Medvedev and Yanukovych and ratified by the two parliaments, extending the lease on Russia's Black Sea Fleet by 25 years until 2043. The presence of the Black Sea Fleet restricts Ukrainian sovereignty and can be used as a pressure point if intergovernmental relations deteriorate. Both Ukraine and Moldova are now in a similar position of having declared their neutrality while Russian troops remain on their territories.

Since assuming the presidency, Yanukovych has initiated policies to speed up security cooperation with Russia, while downgrading the importance of Kiev's ties with NATO.[17] Ukrainian-Russian security cooperation has developed in three areas. First, Moscow and Kiev have reduced their rivalry in the international arms market. Yanukovych has established a new arms export agency, Ukroboronprom, which increased presidential control over arms export policies and tightened integration with the Russian military-industrial complex.

Second, joint ventures between Ukrainian and Russian companies have grown, especially in aircraft and shipbuilding. The Russian Navy's stationing along Ukraine's Black Sea coast is being extended, and Moscow plans to supply new vessels to the Black Sea Fleet. Third, Ukraine and Russia have increased their cooperation in countries that were traditional markets for Soviet arms, such as India, and new Russian markets, such as Iran.

Russia's Deputy Prime Minister Igor Shuvalov has asserted that Ukraine needs to economically integrate with Russia. The chairman of Russia's parliamentary Committee on Economic Policy, Yevgeny Fyodorov, proposed that Ukraine join the Russia-Belarus Union, and Putin himself has invited Ukraine into the Russia-centered CU. Medvedev also invited Kiev into the CSTO, despite its declaration of nonbloc status. Kiev has thus far ruled out CSTO membership and was not prepared to alter its CIS status from observer to full member. Membership in the CU or any of the other economic initiatives has also been resisted, as it would curtail Kiev's control over the country's trade and economic policy.

Some analysts believe that Ukraine's choice is not between Russia and the West, but whether Ukraine joins the European mainstream or is relegated to the European periphery. It may not be Ukraine's preference to move closer to Russia, but Moscow's choice will prevail if Ukraine fails in its gradual integration with the EU. The ultimate choice facing Kiev is between the "shared sovereignty" model of the EU and the "surrendered sovereignty" model of the Eurasian bloc. Ukraine is unlikely to devise and survive an effective "third way" through its self-declared nonbloc status.

In the long term, the Kremlin seeks to permanently alter Ukraine's foreign policy, guarantee a Russia-friendly regime, stifle the country's aspirations to join Western institutions, and ensure Ukraine's permanent neutrality. Putin may be satisfied with the Belarusanization of Ukraine as long as this does not precipitate a destabilizing social upheaval. But unlike with Belarus, in Ukraine public opinion, anti-authoritarianism and counter-Kremlin sentiments are more visible, and a tightening Russian corset is likely to provoke a strong reaction against President Yanukovych and against Moscow, whether through elections or extra-parliamentary revolt.

TARGET BELARUS

The tug of war between Russia and the West over the future of Belarus appears to be reaching a climax. Instead of performing a balancing act between Russia and the West, President Alyaksandr Lukashenka has been slipping from the tightrope and heading toward a hard landing in the Russian net. While the West demands democracy and does not guarantee Lukashenka the levers of power, Moscow pursues control over key sectors of the economy and tolerates his remaining in power. As EU sanctions have intensified because of political repression, Minsk depends even more on Russian loans and purchases.

Russia's economic buy-out of Belarus has been accelerating during the past year. The sale of state assets was a key condition of a bailout package that helped Belarus avoid economic collapse after the 2011 currency crisis. In return for subsidized gas, the cheapest in Europe ($164 per 1,000 cubic meters in 2012), Minsk has lost full control over the country's pipeline to Russia. Belarusian authorities have sold industrial assets worth $2.5 billion in order to receive the third tranche of the $3 billion stabilization loan issued by the EEC in June 2011. Moscow and Minsk have also signed deals for approximately $20 billion in Russian purchases, price concessions, and credits between 2012 and 2015, a figure that amounts to nearly half of Belarus' gross domestic product (GDP).

The privatization plan entails a complete or partial selling of key Belarusian companies to Russian tycoons, even though Minsk continues to resist major acquisitions of its prized assets.[18] Nonetheless, Europe's largest refinery, Belarus's Naftan, may soon be sold to Russia's Lukoil. Minsk has been offered full-scale Russian support in the event of tighter Western sanctions, while Lukashenka has called for intensifying military-political cooperation within the CSTO.[19] Such developments may actually suit Brussels and Washington, which prefer that Belarus become a Russian concern and no longer a Western problem.

Moscow, especially with the triumphal return of Putin to the Kremlin and his vision of a EurU, will certainly not want Lukashenka replaced with an unpredictable and unruly democrat. Ideally, the Kremlin would welcome a more amenable and less abrasive government in Minsk that can help Putin, while providing lucrative benefits for Russia's FSB tycoons. But short of that, Moscow will tacitly support a Lukashenka presidency if Putin continues to keep the West at a firm distance.

At the same time, the military union between the two capitals is being consolidated.[20] In February 2009, Moscow and Minsk signed an agreement on the joint protection of the Russia-Belarus Union State's airspace and the creation of an integrated regional air defense network. The network is expected to comprise five air force units, 10 air defense units, five technical service and support units, and one electronic warfare unit.

Political planners in Moscow are fearful of Arab-type revolutions anywhere in their neighborhood, as they could prove contagious in Russia. In claiming an "area of responsibility" that coincides with the defunct Soviet Union, Moscow is developing several contingencies where military intervention would be warranted. For instance, the organization may become directly involved if the head of the state is cornered by the domestic opposition and requests CSTO assistance. In such a scenario, the CSTO could intervene to protect the "constitutional order," in other words, to help subdue social or ethnic unrest. The Russian General Staff is reportedly accelerating preparations for creating CSTO forces on standby for possible intervention, and such missions would not require approval by the United Nations (UN) Security Council.

Belarus would be an obvious target of Moscow's plans and may welcome a brotherly CSTO intervention if President Lukashenka's position is endangered.

Even more troublesome, some EU members may actually favor CSTO involvement and a Russian-led peacekeeping force to stabilize Belarus. Additionally, the replacement of Lukashenka by a more pliable pro-Russian leader could be acceptable in Brussels, and Moscow is unlikely to be ostracized for replacing the often-described "last dictator in Europe."

TARGET MOLDOVA

While the overriding priority of the current Moldovan government is European integration, Moscow wants to keep the country outside both NATO and the EU and to enroll it in its own integrationist structures. The Kremlin uses several factors to maintain pressure on Chisinau; above all, it manipulates the separatist Transnistrian conflict.

International negotiations over Transnistria recently restarted after almost 6 years. However, Russia's Foreign Minister Sergei Lavrov made it clear that any reunification of Moldova would be conditional.[21] Any "federal" setup would require Russian arbitration, agreement, and troop presence, with a guaranteed special status for Transnistria, enabling it to veto Chisinau's foreign and security policymaking. According to Lavrov, Moldova's foreign policy decisions should reflect its permanent neutrality as inscribed in its constitution. Moldova's EU integration is allegedly incompatible with the country's permanent neutrality and its close relations with Russia. Indeed, such interpretations of neutrality are the major condition for any resolution of Transnistrian separatism.

Yevgeny Shevchuk's election as President of Transnistria in December 2011 may actually strengthen Moscow's hand during a new cycle of international negotiations over the territory. Shevchuk believes that

194

Transnistria is a separate state and favors its integration with the Russian Federation. During Russia's presidential elections, Shevchuk urged Transnistria's residents with Russian citizenship to vote for Putin and supported his idea to create a EurU. Additionally, Russia has issued an estimated 150,000 passports to residents of Transnistria.

Russia seeks to legitimize Transnistria's leadership, while Shevchuk's track record is one of consistent loyalty to Russia, the country of his citizenship.[22] Although he has been hailed in Brussels as a potential reformer, Moscow's approach will leave Shevchuk with little room to maneuver. On March 21, 2012, Medvedev appointed Russia's former envoy to NATO, Dmitry Rogozin, as Special Representative of the Russian President for Transnistria.[23] Meanwhile, Prime Minister Putin also appointed Rogozin as chairman of the Russian side of the Russia-Moldova intergovernmental cooperation commission. Rogozin's assignment will cover both local issues and the international negotiating process; he will apparently be reporting to Putin on Transnistria and to Russia's new Prime Minister Medvedev on Russia-Moldova issues.

Rogozin's dual appointment seems designed to treat the two parts of Moldova separately and contribute to legitimizing and institutionalizing the country's division and heighten its dependence on Russia. Rogozin has revealed that Moscow is not only planning to keep its peacekeeping forces in Transnistria, but it also intends to rearm and upgrade them.[24] It may also deploy a radar system in Transnistria, establish a military base, and position Iskander missiles as an alleged response to U.S. missile defense plans and the creation of U.S. bases in Romania.[25] Moldova will thereby become more closely entwined in Russia's integrationist agenda.

IMPACT ON CENTRAL-EASTERN EUROPE

Since the collapse of the Soviet bloc, Russian leaders envisaged post-communist Central-Eastern Europe (CEE) as a string of neutral and weak states, regardless of their internal political structure and economic makeup. A primary Kremlin objective was to prevent these countries from moving into NATO and further diminishing Moscow's strategic maneuverability. The Kremlin sought the region's demilitarization and neutralization so that it would form a buffer between NATO and the CIS. Once Moscow understood that it could not prevent NATO's absorption of the CEE countries, it embarked on a three-pronged approach: containment, division, and marginalization.

First, Russia's administration focused on building a firewall around the former Soviet republics of Ukraine, Belarus, and Moldova to restrict CEE influence and undercut any aspirations among the three capitals to join Western institutions. Second, the Kremlin sought a role in alliance decisionmaking by influencing governments in key states and promoting divisions to weaken NATO's effectiveness. Third, Russia's leaders endeavored to marginalize the CEE states by creating bilateral disputes and depicting them as disruptive "Russophobes" within both NATO and the EU.

In recent years, Moscow has courted Poland as a regional partner, and Warsaw has reciprocated for several reasons. For the Polish government, cordial ties with Moscow boost Poland's stature inside the EU, whose major states such as Germany and France seek closer relations with Russia regardless of its poor human rights record, democratic reversals, and imperial approach toward post-Soviet neighbors. Poland no longer wants to be perceived as a "Russophobic" troublemaker, an image that reduces its influence within the EU. Lessened U.S. involvement with NATO enlargement and with European affairs more generally under the Obama presidency has also contributed to convincing Polish policymakers that Warsaw needs to primarily strengthen its position within the EU. Russia is also seen a sizable market for growing Polish exports and a potential destination for Polish investments.

Moscow views Poland as a rising power within the EU and has therefore offered closer business and energy connections to increase Russia's influence. The Kremlin calculates that improved contacts will prevent Warsaw from blocking EU-Russian initiatives as it has in the past. It would also constrain Warsaw in pushing for the incorporation of the post-Soviet states in Western institutions. Additionally, the prospective importance of Poland as a shale gas producer may transform it into a potential energy competitor with Russia. Hence, Moscow seeks to be part of the development process for new sources of energy and to more closely tie Warsaw into its energy exporting networks.

Paradoxically, Poland's aspirations to become a major EU player and to develop ties with Russia have created an appearance of detachment toward smaller neighbors. Critics of Poland's foreign policy perceive the government of Prime Minister Donald Tusk as intent on placating Russia, Germany, and France to the detriment of other neighborhood relations. If Warsaw significantly reduces its attention toward bordering states, this could prove strategically counterproductive and would serve Moscow's interests.[26] For instance, the ongoing dispute between Warsaw and

Vilnius over the linguistic and educational rights of the Polish minority in Lithuania clearly benefits Moscow's regional "divide and rule" strategy.

In addition, the EU's EaP program toward the European post-Soviet states has lost momentum during the past 2 years. Partnership countries complain that the funds allocated by the EU have not been serious and fail to focus on specific and practical projects. The EaP is in danger of losing the attention of political elites, despite Warsaw's attempts to raise it to the top of the EU agenda and to involve a broad array of EU capitals.

Unresigned to full Baltic sovereignty, Russia's leaders have sought to place Estonia, Latvia, and Lithuania in an undefined "neutral zone" between NATO and the CIS and between Central Europe and Russia. In this way, NATO influences would be minimized, and Russia's expansive national interests safeguarded. During the past 20 years, Moscow has experienced several disappointments in its Baltic policy. It failed to draw the three independent states into a Russian security orbit, and it proved unable to prevent them from moving westward politically and establishing close relations with the United States. The Kremlin was left with a defensive policy of curtailing the influence of the Baltic States on other former Soviet republics. The Kremlin's policy of marginalization and isolation continues. Numerous forms of pressure within Russia's foreign policy arsenal have been applied against the three Baltic countries.

As the major energy supplier to the region, Moscow has periodically sought to disrupt the Baltic economies in order to apply direct pressure and gain political advantage. As a result, each government has tried to limit its dependence on Russia and its susceptibility to blackmail. Moscow also endeavors to control energy transit routes, as this is both financially and politically profitable. Energy supplies are used as leverage to purchase shares in local refining and transportation systems. Periodic threats to reduce or halt supplies are a means of extracting concessions to allow for Russian investments in the local economies.

Moscow aims to convert overwhelming dependence on Russian energy supplies and economic investments into long-term intergovernmental influence. This can provide Moscow with substantial involvement in a targeted country's financial, trade, and investment policies. Russian enterprise officials also gain political influence through engagement with government officials, political parties, interest groups, and media outlets in targeted states.

Russia's officials periodically threaten the Baltic countries, claiming that Estonia, Latvia, and Lithuania were positioning themselves as alleged launching pads for NATO aggression against Russia.[27] Frequent unauthorized military overflight over Baltic airspace indicates that the Kremlin seeks to intimidate its neighbors and to demonstrate that NATO will not ultimately defend their interests in an armed confrontation with Russia. However, in the past 2 years, NATO has drawn up more concrete defense plans for Poland, Estonia, Latvia, and Lithuania, including guarantees of a NATO military response in case of outside attack. The Baltic governments have also gained more regular NATO military exercises in the region. Deliberations have also intensified over the potential hosting of U.S. and NATO military infrastructure, following the Polish, Romanian, and Czech acceptance of components of the new U.S. missile defense system. Some capitals have also proposed NATO army, air force, and naval bases, together with the reorientation of force structures, to cope with conventional threats.

There have been several reported cases of political subversion in the Baltic region, in which influence has been purchased by Russian businessmen tied to the Kremlin's intelligence services. This policy unseated Lithuania's President Rolandas Paksas in April 2004 and placed other officials under suspicion of collaboration. In Latvia's September 2011 elections, the Kremlin supported the Russian ethnic Harmony Party, calculating that, by entering government, it could sway Latvia's policies in a more pro-Moscow direction. However, although Harmony gained a majority of votes among the Russian-speaking minority, it was left out of the new governing coalition by a combination of ethnic Latvian parties because of fears that it could veer Latvia away from its Western orbit. Russian organizations in Latvia also gathered enough signatures to initiate a referendum on making Russian an official second language, but the initiative was defeated on February 18, 2012, by over 74 percent of Latvian voters.[28]

Moscow has tried to benefit from local political, ethnic, subregional religious, and social turbulence in order to keep each Baltic country off balance. It has exploited the Russian minority question to depict the Baltic governments as failing to meet European standards for minority protection and human rights. The Kremlin claims the right to represent and defend the interests not only of Russian ethnics, but also all "Russian speakers" in order to raise the number of alleged victims of Baltic repression. Claims by officials that the Baltic governments actively discriminated against Russians, despite the conclusions of international human rights organizations, contribute to heightening international tensions. Moscow continues to manipulate the ethnic issue at convenient venues, including UN Human Rights Commission sessions. This raises concerns that a more expansionist regime in Moscow could employ aggressive means to support secessionist movements in all three Baltic states.

CEE also provides opportunities for Russian inroads toward the pan-European and transatlantic institutions through economic, political, and intelligence penetration. Russian officials focus on influencing political decisions in these capitals through a combination of diplomatic pressure, personal and professional contacts, economic enticements, energy blackmail, and outright bribery. Reports regularly surface in Slovakia, Hungary, Bulgaria, and other CEE states that "old comrade" networks continue to operate, based on financial and friendship connections rather than on any steadfast ideological or political convictions. Some socialist and social democrat parties in the CEE, where many of the ex-communists have gravitated, have provided the most beneficial opportunities for Russian penetration. Lucrative business contracts, donations to political campaigns, and the purchase of media outlets enable Moscow to exert political influence and convince key politicians to favor Russian business investments and strategic interests.

During the unfolding Putin presidency, one can expect that an aggressive integrationist approach by Moscow toward the post-Soviet states will be mirrored by a more assertive policy toward the CEE countries based around economic entrapment and political neutralization. Any successes registered in reintegrating the European post-Soviet countries within a Eurasian economic, political, and security alliance will also encourage Moscow to pursue a more intrusive policy toward its former CEE satellites in seeking to maneuver them closer to a Russian orbit. This will, in turn, heighten tensions and exacerbate conflicts between Moscow and several Central European capitals.

ENDNOTES - CHAPTER 5

1. Konstantin von Eggert, "Due West: Putin Signals Foreign Policy Shift," *RIA Novosti*, May 18, 2012.

2. Nikolas K. Gvosdev, "The New Russian Empire," *The National Interest*, April 16, 2012, available from *nationalinterest.org/commentary/the-new-ussr-6783*.

3. Previous analyses of Russia's neoimperial ambitions during the first two Putin presidencies can be found in Janusz Bugajski, *Georgian Lessons: Conflicting Russian and Western Interests in the Wider Europe*, Washington, DC: Center for Strategic and International Studies (CSIS) Press, 2010; Janusz Bugajski, *Dismantling the West: Russia's Atlantic Agenda*, Herndon, VA: Potomac Books, 2009; Janusz Bugajski, *Expanding Eurasia: Russia's European Ambitions*, Washington, DC: CSIS Press, 2008; and Janusz Bugajski, *Cold Peace: Russia's New Imperialism*, Westport, CT: Praeger/Greenwood, 2004.

4. For debates on questions of multipolarity and hegemony, see, among others, the website of Russia's International Eurasian Movement and the author's interview on May 14, 2012, available from *evrazia.org/article/1980*.

5. Available from *telegraf.by/en/2012/04/putin-pogovoril-s-lukashenko-ob-integracii-v-ramkah-eep*.

6. "Russia Remakes the CSTO," *Stratfor: Geopolitical Diary*, February 16, 2012, available from *www.stratfor.com/geopolitical-diary/russia-remakes-csto*.

7. Available from *sudevrazes.org/en/main.aspx?guid=18021&detail=67083*.

8. "Does Putin's Return To Kremlin Breathe New Life Into Eurasian Union Project?" Radio Free Europe/Radio Liberty, March 6, 2012, available from *www.rferl.org/content/putin_eurasian_union_cis/24506282.html*.

9. See Anders Aslund, "Putin's Eurasian Illusion Will Lead to Isolation," *The Moscow Times*, June 21, 2012.

10. For a valuable analysis of Russia's imperial mindset toward Ukraine, see Alexander Bogomolov and Oleksandr Lytvynenko, "A Ghost in the Mirror: Russian Soft Power in Ukraine," London, UK: Chatham House, January 2012, available from *www.chathamhouse.org/sites/default/files/public/Research/Russia%20and%20Eurasia/0112bp_bogomolov_lytvynenko.pdf*.

11. Available from *www.bloomberg.com/news/2012-06-05/ukrainian-parliament-approves-language-bill-amid-protests.html*.

12. Oleksandr Kramar, "Russification Redux?" *The Ukrainian Weekly*, International Ed., No. 9, Issue 32, Kiev, Ukraine, June 2012, p. 5. Since this writing, the language law has become accepted as part of Ukrainian law by the Rada.

13. Taras Kuzio, "Russia Takes Control of Ukraine's Security Forces," *Eurasia Daily Monitor*, March 19, 2012, Vol. 9, Issue 55. Khoroshkovsky, long regarded as a Russian agent of influence in the Yanukovych administration, moved from the Ukrainian Security Service (SBU) to serve briefly as Finance Minister and to the important position of First Deputy Prime Minister. Khoroshkovsky was believed to be behind numerous scandals in 2010-11, when he headed the SBU that undermined Ukraine's European integration. The appointments have removed the security forces from under the control of the oligarchs and placed them directly under President Yanukovych and Moscow's supervision. Their primary responsibility will be to defend Yanukovych and ensure his re-election. With Yanukovych acquiescing to Russian influence over the security forces, Putin evidently has a personal stake in maintaining Yanukovych in power.

14. Kateryna Choursina, "Ukrainian Parliament Backs Bill to Ban Sale of Gas Pipelines," April 13, 2012 , available from *www.bloomberg.com/news/print/2012-04-13/ukrainian-parliament-backs-bill-to-ban-sale-of-gas-pipelines.html*.

15. "Ukraine to Reduce Gas Purchases from Russia - Yanukovych," *RIA Novosti*, Kiev, Ukraine, March 6, 2012, available from *en.ria.ru/business/20120306/171791981.html*.

16. Olga Shumylo-Tapiola, "Ukraine and Russia: Another Gas War?" February 21, 2012, Washington, DC: Carnegie Endowment, 2012, available from *carnegieendowment.org/2012/02/21/ukraine-and-russia-another-gas-war/9roh*.

17. Taras Kuzio, "Growing Ukrainian-Russian Arms Export Cooperation," *Eurasia Daily Monitor*, May 15, 2012, Vol. 9, Issue 92.

18. Grigory Ioffe, "Belarus: A Death Penalty, A Standoff With The EU And A Drift Toward Russia," *Eurasia Daily Monitor*, March 21, 2012, Vol. 9, Issue 57. Among the 19 enterprises are BelAZ (which produces heavy trucks for mining operations, controls 30 percent of the world market for these trucks), MAZ (trucks), and MKZT (heavy-duty tractor-trailers to transport ballistic missiles).

19. "Belarus, Russia Need to Step up Military-Technical Cooperation - Lukashenko," *Russia & CIS Military Newswire*, March 1, 2012.

20. "Russia to Deliver More Air Defense Systems to Belarus," Minsk, Moscow, April 18, 2012, *RIA Novosti*, available from *en.ria.ru/world/20120418/172899923.html*.

21. Vladimir Socor, "Lavrov Squashes Hope For Constructive Restart Of Transnistria Negotiations," *Eurasia Daily Monitor*, November 29, 2011, Vol. 8, Issue 216.

22. Vladimir Socor, "Too Early For A Political Investment In Transnistria's Shevchuk," *Eurasia Daily Monitor*, March 9, 2012, Vol. 9, Issue 49. Shevchuk's statements have called for preparing Transnistria's accession to the Commonwealth of Independent States (CIS) Customs Union (CU), and the Eurasian Union (EurU), adopting the Russian ruble for parallel circulation with the Transnistrian "ruble," and pursuing the "Eastern vector of Transnistria's development."

23. Vladimir Socor, "Dmitry Rogozin Appointed Special Presidential Representative For Transnistria," *Eurasia Daily Monitor,* March 23, 2012, Vol. 9, Issue 59.

24. Dan Peleschuk, "The Patron State," *Russia Profile*, April 17, 2012, available from *russiaprofile.org/international/57617.html.* Russia maintains a motorized infantry battalion in Transnistria as part of the Collective Peacekeeping Forces in addition to a number of troops guarding several Soviet-era ammunition depots.

25. "Russia to Deploy Missile Defense Radar in Transnistria," *Sofia News Agency,* April 17, 2012, available from *www.novinite. com/view_news.php?id=138577.*

26. See Janusz Bugajski, "Poland's Progress: Where Warsaw Fits in Europe," *Current History: A Journal of Contemporary World Affairs,* Vol. 110, Issue 734, March 2011.

27. For an overview of Russia's pressures on the Baltic states, see Bugajski, *Dismantling the West,* pp. 96-99.

28. "Latvians Say No in Russian Language Vote," February 19, 2012, available from *www.euronews.net.*

ABOUT THE CONTRIBUTORS

HARLEY BALZER is a Professor in the Department of Government and School of Foreign Service, and an Associated Faculty member of the History Department at Georgetown University. In 1992-93, he served as Executive Director and Chairman of the Board of the International Science Foundation, George Soros's largest program to aid the former Soviet Union. Dr. Balzer's research interests include comparative authoritarianism, focusing on Russia and China; science and technology; education; and social history. His publications include *Soviet Science on the Edge of Reform* (1989); *Five Years That Shook the World: Gorbachev's Unfinished Revolution* (1991), which was named a CHOICE outstanding academic book; and *Russia's Missing Middle Class: The Professions in Russian History* (1996). Current writing projects include a comparative study of Russian and Chinese interaction with the global economy; a book on current Russian politics; a monograph on the expansion of Russian higher education in the Tsarist era, Soviet Union, and Post-Soviet Russia; and a study of the middle class after communism.

STEPHEN J. BLANK served as the Strategic Studies Institute's expert on the Soviet bloc and the post-Soviet world from 1989 to 2013. Prior to that, he was Associate Professor of Soviet Studies at the Center for Aerospace Doctrine, Research, and Education, Maxwell Air Force Base, AL; he taught at the University of Texas, San Antonio; and he taught at the University of California, Riverside. Dr. Blank is the editor of *Imperial Decline: Russia's Changing Position in Asia*, coeditor of *Soviet Military and the Future*, and author of *The Sorcerer as Apprentice: Stalin's Commissariat of Nationali-*

ties, 1917-1924. He has also written many articles and conference papers on Russia, the Commonwealth of Independent States, and Eastern European security issues. Dr. Blank's current research deals with proliferation and the revolution in military affairs, and energy and security in Eurasia. His two most recent books are *Russo-Chinese Energy Relations: Politics in Command,* London, UK: Global Markets Briefing, 2006; and *Natural Allies? Regional Security in Asia and Prospects for Indo-American Strategic Cooperation* (Carlisle, PA: Strategic Studies Institute, U.S. Army War College, 2005). Dr. Blank holds a B.A. in history from the University of Pennsylvania, and an M.A. and Ph.D. in history from the University of Chicago.

JANUSZ BUGAJSKI is a policy analyst, author, lecturer, columnist, consultant, and television host based in the United States. His current positions include Senior Associate at the Center for Strategic and International Studies and host of the television show "Bugajski Hour," broadcast on Albanian Screen from Tirana, Albania. Mr. Bugajski is the author of 18 books on Europe, Russia, and transatlantic relations; is a regular contributor to various U.S. and European newspapers; publishes in international journals; and is a columnist for media outlets in Albania, Bosnia-Herzegovina, Bulgaria, Croatia, Georgia, Kosova, and Ukraine. Mr. Bugajski's forthcoming book is entitled *Conflict Zones: North Caucasus and Western Balkans Compared* (Washington DC: Jamestown Foundation, 2014).

STEFAN HEDLUND is Professor at the Centre for Russian and Eurasian Studies at Uppsala University, Sweden. Trained as an economist, he has specialized in

Russian affairs since the final days of Leonid Brezhnev in the early 1980s. Over the years, his research interests have branched far outside economics to include, above all, a great interest in Russian history. He has traveled and lectured widely, in academic as well as business contexts, enjoying two sabbatical semesters at Harvard University and shorter stays as visiting scholar in academic institutions that range from Stanford University, California, to Hokkaido University, Japan, and various places in Washington, DC. Mr. Hedlund has published extensively on matters ranging from the Soviet system, to post-Soviet transition, and institutional dimensions of the interaction between state and market in a modern economy, including more than 20 books, 200 journal and magazine articles, and well over 300 reviews and op-ed pieces. His latest monograph is *Invisible Hands, Russian Experience and Social Science: Approaches to Understanding Systemic Failure* (Cambridge University Press, 2011). He is currently finishing a book on Russian energy policy, which will be published by Lynne Rienner Publishers.

STEVEN ROSEFIELDE is Professor of Economics at the University of North Carolina, Chapel Hill, a member of the Russian Academy of Natural Sciences and former Director of the Japan foundation Project on the Global Financial Crisis's Impact on Asia. His most recent books include *Russia in the 21st Century: The Prodigal Superpower* (Cambridge University Press, 2005); *Masters of Illusion* (with Quinn Mills, Cambridge University Press, 2007); *Russian Economy* (Wiley, 2008); *Russia Since 1980: Wrestling With Westernization* (with Stefan Hedlund, Cambridge University Press, 2009); *Red Holocaust* (Routledge, 2010); *Two Asias: The Emerging Postcrisis Divide* (ed. with Masaaki Kuboniwa and

Satoshi Mizobata, World Scientific, 2012); *Prevention and Crisis Management: Lessons for Asia from the 2008 Crisis* (ed. with Masaaki Kuboniwa and Satoshi Mizobata, World Scientific, 2012); *Democracy and its Elected Enemies* (with Quinn Mills, Cambridge University Press, 2013); and *Asian Economic Systems* (World Scientific, 2013).

www.ingramcontent.com/pod-product-compliance
Lightning Source LLC
Chambersburg PA
CBHW080245290526
45790CB00005B/1714